Butterfly Wings

Sue Williams

(Shalom 4)

email: chosen1@ntlworld.com

Printed by Kindle Print
Also available on Amazon for Kindle
Cover: Diyan Kantardzhiev

E-mail: diyan@innovation-photography.co.uk

Taken from the original painting by Artist Dawn Fisher

www.dawnfisherart.uk Email: dawn@dawnfisherart.uk

Some names have been changed in this book to protect their identity.

Scripture quotations taken from the New International Version (NIV), Good News Bible and The Message.

All royalties from this book will be donated to the Care Fund at Parklands Church, Swansea.

About the Author

Sue Williams (aka Mama Sue) is a speaker, hospice chaplaincy volunteer, pastoral worker as well as a quirky and zany creative. She has a heart for people and a fierce love for Jesus that shines through in all that she does. As a widow who has had seasons of caring for loved ones, she has ministered to weary ladies for decades through various means. Whether through speaking at events, hosting her biannual TLC days for ladies or the ministry of Shalom4, her home which provides short term respite, her life is testament to God's amazing grace and compassion that she exudes to all she meets. Sue is mother, step-mother, grandmother and great grandmother. At 75, her vibrance and energy is an inspiration to many, young and old.

Acknowledgements

I would like to thank those who took time to write in the reviews and inspired me to take another leap of faith to write this sequel to *This is My Story, This is My Song*. My sincere thanks to my lovely proofreader, who wishes to remain anonymous. You are an absolute darling! To Dawn and Diyan for their hard work in the production of its lovely cover. To Ann Thomas for all the work in getting this book through the publishing process. To those who have allowed me to tell their stories. My special thanks to the three couples who had the courage to allow themselves to relive their most painful times so that you, the readers, might see the faithfulness of a loving God in their lives. And to you, the reader, for buying this book. May you grow closer to Jesus through the pages of this book: *Butterfly Wings*.

CONTENTS

Sue Williams has written this book in response to a word God clearly gave her: ***Tell of what I have done for you***. The scripture He gave her was from Psalm 9: *I'm thanking you God from a full heart. I'm writing the book of your wonders. I'm whistling, laughing and jumping for joy. I'm singing your song, High God.* (The Message)

May you be encouraged and even challenged to launch out into the deep, abandoning your comfort zone, setting your sails to new horizons as you embrace the love and provision of Jesus in a way you never thought possible. I promise you that if you do, you will never be the same…

This is My Story, This is My Song - reviewed in the United Kingdom on 23rd November 2020.

This is a beautiful account of the joys and trials of an ordinary life, lived for a higher purpose. Sue's story demonstrates the immeasurably positive impact on others, of a life lived in simple obedience to God. Sue's experience of following Jesus in a context of much suffering and loss is authentic, powerful and overwhelmingly inspirational. Sue speaks with such passion and energy, a gently challenging but genuinely motivational read. Thank you, Sue, for being faithful to God's call on your life, and for sharing yourself so generously with others, in reality, and within the pages of this book. It's been a joy. I eagerly await the sequel!

Jan M.

PREFACE

It's nearly two years now since I wrote my first book, *This is My Story, This is My Song.* Its journey through the platform of Amazon Kindle ebook followed by a published paperback by Amazon still doesn't fail to amaze me.

I believe that the Lord wanted me to share all that He's done for me as a testimony of His loving kindness to me and those who know and love Him.

As I peeped through the reviews and saw the kind words being said, I felt content that I had finally done what God had asked. An air of satisfaction filled me. Job done. I can breathe out. But wait, what was that they were asking for – a sequel? Oh, surely not.

I began to list in my mind numerous reasons why I couldn't possibly write a sequel. I groaned and tried to dismiss the idea. I dialogued with God, putting my case forward with all my answers, ready to give reasons not to do it: 'I've said all I thought You wanted me to say, Lord, and in any case it looks like life at present will be mostly in the confines of my home and garden, even as lockdown eases. 'Draw from your memories!' That word began to set like concrete in my mind. Maybe this was the beginning of foundations for a sequel. You've got to lead me, Lord!

During the day I let thoughts process in my mind reflecting on the reasons why there was a call to do a sequel. Some readers wanted more. More stories of what God had done. There seemed a hunger to hear more about the God who can work in the mundane as well as the miraculous. The authentic stories of real people who have seen the hand of God swoop into their lives and change them forever, giving them renewed hope and a future.

I reached for my iPad to open a document, in faith believing that if this is what He wanted, He will surely do it again and guide my hand every step of the way.

At the time I'd just had a plaster cast removed from my broken right hand following a fall that also caused a nasty leg injury. So with splinted fingers I began to type with my left hand… well, here goes, Lord…over to You...

I looked up the word 'sequel' to make sure I had full understanding of the word: 'a published, broadcast or recorded work that continues the story or develops the theme of an earlier one'. OK I get it. I just may be able to do this…with the Lord's help, of course.

My delight to hear that in my first book many of the readers reviewed and said that they felt they were in my home with me, relaxed, and it was as if they were sitting in my living room with me as I shared my stories. That's exactly what I want to achieve in this book, *Butterfly Wings*.

I must confess that even during the Covid lockdowns when I had the time and could have got the sequel written and finished, I did not feel motivated to do so.

I'm praying that this is now God's timing.

So, get yourself your favourite hot drink, your comfy chair and put your feet up. May you feel relaxed, refreshed and challenged as you read more of the loving kindness of Jesus.

1
BUTTERFLY WINGS

What a strange title you may think if you haven't read my first book. I need to tell you that butterflies are very special to me. My apologies to those who already know my story of why butterflies are precious to me. For those who don't know, I will share with you later in this chapter.

But first let's look at the lifespan of a peacock butterfly. I must confess I knew very little about the life of a butterfly. Let me take a few moments to share with you some research I did.

I was particularly interested in the beautiful peacock butterfly with its majestic vibrant markings. The British butterfly hibernates to escape our cold and windy winters. As it prepares to hibernate, it converts some of its blood sugar into glycerol to act like a form of anti-freeze in readiness for the coming winter. It finds sheltered places like a tree with holes or even our garden sheds. When settled, it will tuck itself into its wings and sleep. The only thing visible is the dark underside, making itself less conspicuous and safe in its temporary environment.

Spring arrives, the temperatures begin to rise and because of its successful hibernation it begins to appear on the sunny days of March. As it emerges, its first task is to look for food – its first meal of the year.

We see its magnificent colourful eye-spots and upper wings and marvel at its beauty. But there is more; its beauty is also a means of defence. If it gets disturbed the peacock butterfly can rub its wings together and make a hissing sound; this, combined with its large eye-spots, will keep predators at bay.

Over the next warmer months the butterfly lays its eggs, as many as 500 at a time, on the underside of stinging nettle leaves. As they are laid in layers it decreases the chance of making a tasty meal for the birds.

As weeks go by the adult butterfly, having lived nearly a year, will die. But all is not lost. The caterpillars of the next generation hatch, tucking into the nettle leaves for strength. In July they form into chrysalises and are reborn as adult peacock butterflies in August, the cycle completed.

You might say to me, 'fascinating, but what has that to do with me?' Let me tell you about the butterfly God brought to speak to me. I was walking on the beautiful Gower beach of Rhossili with its three-mile stretch of magnificent coastline. I was walking toward the little island of Burry Holms. (Its history goes back to the Middle Stone Age. Latterly it was the home of ecclesiastical monks during medieval times.)

As I walked along the beach to the sea, I noticed that the sea had foam produced by the algae. Then I spotted a beautiful butterfly caught up in this foam and unable to move. I grabbed a large shell I found on the sand and scooped up the butterfly. Slowly I walked to a nearby pool. A feather was lying on the sand so I began dipping the feather into the clear water of the pool and very gingerly began to gently wash its wings and release it from the clinging grey sea foam.

I decided that I needed to place it in some greenery, so I put the dripping butterfly, which was still on the shell, rested it in the shelter of my trainer and proceeded to walk to the greenery in the distance. When I got there I placed the butterfly in its natural habitat and felt satisfied that I had done all I could to help it.

As I turned to continue my walk to Burry Holms, I felt the Lord saying to me, 'That's what I want you do to for Me. I will send you those whose colour has gone because of all they've been through. I want you to bathe them gently with TLC, then let them fly again.'

This was the ministry the Lord was lending me…broken lives through pain and suffering, loss, grief, sickness, abuse, rejection, divorce, all that would make a once beautiful creation, like that butterfly, lose its once vibrant beautiful colours, turning it into dull, lifeless grey.

As you begin to read through the pages, I want you to picture a canvas. A butterfly shape has been drawn on it. It fills the canvas, but it is grey.

I pray that each chapter with its challenge and prayer will be a brushstroke of new God-colour in your life, to inspire you, encourage you, and lead you nearer to Jesus.

2
GOD OF THE CHIP SHOP

Let me give you a full picture of the backdrop of this very special day in my life that I will never forget 31st October, 2008. I will set the scene: over an eighteen-month period between caring for my late dad's needs, I began tackling a very high overgrown hedge, laboriously cutting it down to a manageable size. It had grown out of all proportion and was impossible to trim unless I precariously balanced on a ladder whilst grabbing a branch with the other hand and holding on for dear life. I progressed from loppers to an electric saw, although a chainsaw was prohibited for me. I wonder why!

Weeks turned to months, and I worked through the seasons until I was left with bare privet bushes that looked more like they had been stripped by a swarm of locusts. One thing was for sure they were now manageable!

The spare ground that was surrounded by the hedges had become overgrown too. For years when my dad was fit and able, he planted fruit bushes and we also had lots of fresh vegetables from the fruit of his labour. Now it was overgrown, full of brambles that gave it the appearance of being unloved, unkempt and totally unmanageable.

As I cut down this hedge, I piled and piled the branches on this plot. Winter came. Spring followed and new growth began growing through this mound of cut-off branches. Summer began. I made enquires of ways to have it taken away, but decided after hearing the extortionate cost that ran into a few hundred pounds, it was time to have a new plan.

I began working for weeks and weeks sawing them to size, making every branch car-friendly so that they could be taken to our local recycling area. Catherine, whom I mentioned in my first book, came to the rescue. We began the mammoth task of filling the boot of her little blue Fiesta over thirty times, taking each load to the recycling plant until we finally had everything cleared.

Can you imagine how I felt? I couldn't have been more elated if I'd climbed Everest without shoes on! The last loads were taken during the afternoon of Friday, 31st October, 2008. I was ecstatic. The work on the hedges over the eighteen months was finally completed. Done!

A Friday custom in our house was a walk to the local chip shop to pick up fish and chips for our dinner. I decided I would go straight from the tip as it was on my route home. Clad in my work clothes, I walked into the chip shop with its intoxicating aroma of freshly-cooking chips and fish. The warmth was welcoming from the cool autumn air outside. I was absorbed in its delicious aroma, reflecting on my long hedge battle. The battle was won. I was lost in my victory.

Voices around me abruptly drew me back into my surroundings. The shop was full of hungry people waiting for their orders. One voice stood out. A tall, strong-looking man, around my age, with a cosmopolitan accent, began telling the lady serving how he remembered a bag of chips costing the old thruppeny bit (the old three pence). I decided not to join in the conversation so as to reveal my age, but as the talk continued about quantities he would need for three portions, I felt obligated to help by confirming with him that the portions were very generous and that he would have plenty in the order that he had chosen.

As he waited for his order, we struck up a conversation. I asked him what was a man from abroad doing in a local Penlan chip shop. He explained he was on vacation following a trip to Eastern Europe and had called to see his family who lived locally. As the conversation continued over the steaming fish and chip counter, I learned that his name was Jack and he had lived in Penlan for most his childhood before going to study at a university abroad.

We talked about the local primary school. Jack said he had gone to Gwyrosydd School. I told him my father, Mr Watson, had taught there. Jack was astonished, saying that he had so much respect for him and was amazed that he was alive and still living in the same house and in his eighties. He shared that as a child he and his friends would come and play near our garden in the hope of catching a glimpse of their beloved teacher. He was their hero. We realised as children we would have been playing in the same school playground, attending the same assemblies. How small had our world become during those moments in the steamy fish and chip shop!

I invited Jack to visit my dad at anytime. He was travelling back home the next day and said when he was in Swansea next he would love to take up the invitation.

I came back with my piping hot bag of fish and chips for our dinner and as we sat enjoying our meal, I excitedly told my father of the chance meeting I had with an ex-pupil of his from over fifty years ago.

As a Christian, I personally don't celebrate Halloween. Other years I would have made some alternative-type treats but because of the amount of work I was doing getting rid of the hedge, time had run out for me to prepare.

The door bell rang. I'd said to my dad that I wasn't going to answer as it would be Halloween callers and I hadn't got anything alternative for them. The door bell persistently rang again. Irritated, I hurried to answer it ready to say no to what I thought would be Halloween-costumed callers demanding a treat.

As I opened the door, ready with my speech why I didn't truck with Halloween, I quickly swallowed my words when I saw it was actually Jack from the chip shop standing there! He'd decided, after talking with his family, to call down for a quick visit before he flew off some hours later.

I invited him in and he and my dad immediately got into conversation. Jack thanked my dad for the impact he had had on his life. In fact, he said that he was a physician and that the very first speech he had made was coached by his much-loved teacher, Mr Watson. It was the story from the Bible of 'The Prodigal Son'.

Dad was delighted and loved answering the many questions that Jack was asking him about his army service as he had a passion for World War 1 and 2 books and memorabilia.

When I think back to that day, I'm sure Jack must have thought I had come from another planet! Because I had experienced such an awesome week in the way God was working out His purposes, I suddenly wondered if perhaps this wasn't just a coincidence meeting him, but indeed a God-incidence.

I clumsily tried to get into their conversation by saying that I went to church. I will never forget the look on his face! It was totally irrelevant to their conversation and the comment promptly sunk into oblivion, or so I thought. After a while I think Jack thought he'd better be polite and asked me about my church. By that time I was wishing the ground would swallow me up. Ever been there?

Dad was delighted to tell Jack that I'd just spent time cataloguing on my laptop his wartime memoirs with photos and accounts, and proudly told him he was in the REME 11th British Liberation Army Armoured Troops Workshop which he headed up, having landed on the French beach a few days after D-Day. He had in fact made and placed the last star on the car of British Field Marshall Bernard Law Montgomery (1887-1976) who was among the most decorated military leaders of World War 2.

Dad then asked if Jack had a business card and said I could email the file to him. Both men were delighted. It was a joy to see Dad so animated. His world had shrunk with his ageing and mobility problems; conversations like this brought life into his mundane day.

We asked Jack about his job and life abroad. It was a light, pleasant conversation. Suddenly, completely out of the blue, I felt this heart pain and burden for him. I knew instantly that this man was deeply troubled, and realised from that minute on that our meeting was not just a coincidence or a chance meeting, but most certainly a God incidence.

I emailed the details as requested which he received on his return home. Little did I know what God had in store…I was about to go on a journey I would never forget.

God had plans. Our communication changed very quickly from being a polite acknowledgement for sending the wartime memory files of his much-respected teacher to a long lasting friendship.

I must admit at this stage I felt God might have made a big mistake. Jack was a well-respected physician, very educated, intelligent and certainly didn't suffer fools gladly. Why would he need or even want to communicate with me? Surely if God wanted to convey and help Jack in any way by bringing an earthly angel alongside him, He would have sent a proficient, intellectual person not a Penlan widow without certificates of achievement on her wall? That's the thing with God isn't it; He uses the most unlikely circumstances and people to bring about His master plan. His ways are most certainly not ours!

The following weeks I began to share with him some

of the amazing things God had done in my life. Jack was wary of me at first, having had negative experiences with some who professed their faith in God. After a time he saw I was a genuine Christian, without any agendas and so he began to trust me and share the struggles and pains that were crippling him. He had a faith in God but there seemed something missing.

We stepped up communications and discovered the joys of Skype and free video linking with FaceTime. As the weeks turned into months and even years of regular contact, we became true friends with a trust we had built up over time. As I was able to support Jack with prayer, a listening ear and advice at times, so he supported me during many difficult years. He became the brother I never had.

We spent hours and hours talking through Bible passages and the concepts of them. Because it was a video link, it made things a lot easier as we could discuss many things together including the struggles life was throwing our way.

During this time God began to show me He had something more for Jack. This was the reality of grace. So many of us spend most of our lives trying to earn our way to God. We are brought up in a society that acceptance is approved of by what we can give. Our achievements bring approval and respect. But when that comes to God, it's different. Of course we should do good works but that is not the means to salvation. The Bible tells us good works…will follow salvation. Salvation is all God's doing.

The only way to God is through Jesus. God sent His Son to die on the cross for me, for you. He took our sins and has given us a way of salvation and freedom, a future and a hope. We have a choice. God never forces Himself on us. He is a loving Heavenly Father and waits patiently for us as He draws us to Himself.

It's all about GRACE – undeserved favour. There are many books out there on grace. When Jack next visited Wales we took a trip to the beautiful Christian retreat at Nicholaston House in Gower where I had become involved as a volunteer. As I showed him around the beautiful grounds and he took in the spectacular panoramic views over the stunning Oxwich Bay, I gave him a new Bible and two books to read on grace – The Grace of God by Andy Stanley and All of Grace by Charles Spurgeon. Charles Haddon Spurgeon (19th June, 1834-31st January, 1892) was an English Particular Baptist preacher. His books down through the ages have been so influential on his teaching of sound doctrine. This book was short, a simply-written book, and to be honest I grappled with giving it to him as I wondered if this would be too basic for his intellect.

He received the books graciously and devoured them. We spent many hours after he returned home discussing the concept of grace, until that day that I will never forget. I knew that God was doing an amazing work in his life, and as he himself expressed later that a paradigm shift occurred.

I witnessed a miracle over the internet that day on this video link. As we continued to speak about grace, I 'saw' a total transformation in Jack. The concept of grace had changed from being just a concept to a reality.

The Spirit of God had enlightened him with nothing short of a revelation of the grace of God. He was changed forever. No longer had he to earn his salvation or his place in Heaven.

What a privilege to have been given this opportunity by God to experience His amazing way in which His love overflows as He reveals Himself to those who call on Him.

Over a decade has passed since this paradigm shift happened in Jack's life. We have journeyed over these years together, mostly by virtual links over the internet and during his frequent visits to Wales until Covid-19.

We have supported one another during times of joys and sorrows, given advice to one another in difficult circumstances, but mostly shared fellowship with one another in Jesus, praying for our families and seeing wonderful answers to our prayers.

I said earlier that Jack was my friend, my brother, and for that I will always be eternally grateful to God for bringing him into my life. The canvas of my life has been given a God-colour, all because of a bag of fish and chips!

From a chrysalis to a butterfly…

Challenge:

Am I in the rut of being stuck in a chrysalis? Do I need to exercise my spiritual wings again?

Prayer:

Lord Jesus, I am encased in this shroud of complacency. Show me how to cast this shroud off so I can be set free and soar once again. Amen.

3
GOD OF THE — DASH

If I asked you what does a dash mean to you, you might react like me and say, 'A dash means rushing from one place to another.' You might use the sentence, 'Sorry, can't stop, I've got to *dash* to the shop before it closes.' Grammatically, it actually means this: 'a dash is longer than a hyphen and is commonly used to indicate a range or a pause.'

The most common types of dashes are the en dash (–) and the em dash (—). I was delighted to discover how to find the dash on my iPad, neatly hidden behind the hyphen symbol on the keyboard. Interesting you may say, but what's it got to do with God?

Let me tell you. A few years ago I was sent a video clip and the title was, 'What are you doing with your dash?' I was intrigued and sat, all ears, watching this short clip. It really spoke to me. In fact, so much so that I sent it to my pastor who shared it and expounded it in a really challenging sermon.

Before I share more about my dash, and maybe we look at yours, I would like to introduce you to a lovely friend of mine called Pam Williams. Let me tell you about her —dash.

Pam is a lady in her late fifties. Pam suffers with a disease called multiple sclerosis. Multiple sclerosis (MS) is a condition that can affect the brain and spinal cord, causing a wide range of potential symptoms, including problems with vision, arm or leg movement, sensation or balance. The immune system attacks the covering of the nerves. Pam has secondary MS which, unless God intervenes, is a downward spiral and she would become more and more disabled.

Over five years ago, after a very low period in her life, Pam moved home to a new location and a purpose-built complex that could provide facilities to make her life a little easier. This so happened to be next door to Parklands church which I attend.

Pam is a Christian and had been active in Christian service especially in the field of administration for many years. An attractive, efficient, capable young lady, her passion and her faith in Jesus shone through her. I will never forget our first meeting. I rang the bell connected to her flat and she activated the outside doors to let me in. I followed her instructions and took the lift to the next floor and made my way to her front door.

I was greeted by this beautiful woman, tall and elegant, her long hair shining. She was immaculately dressed. She managed with some difficulty to walk and greeted me at the door with the help of electrodes attached to her foot. These helped her lift her foot to walk. Functional Electrical Stimulation (FES) is a treatment that applies small electrical charges to a muscle that has become paralysed or weak. In MS it is mostly used as a treatment for foot drop, where disruptions in the nerve pathways between the legs and brain mean the front of her foot cannot be lifted to the correct angle when walking.

I immediately admired the determination of this beautiful young lady as she welcomed me into her beautifully-furnished lounge. Her smile and eagerness to share her story was apparent. There was a presence of peace around her that was almost tangible. I glanced around her light and airy, inviting, neat room and could see various pieces of equipment used to aid her with her physical disability.

Pam began to share how she had become very depressed as the MS had begun to progress. Her living accommodation at the time in another area of Swansea had become unsuitable and her well-being had become seriously compromised. She was very unwell and very depressed which led her to attempt suicide which, to the astonishment of the medics, failed. This in itself was a miracle considering she had taken so many pills.

Pam was discharged from hospital with a support team who knew there had to be changes for her to be able to carry on. They told her of Hazel Court complex at Sketty. Enquiries were made and eventually a tenancy was offered on an apartment in this modern, purpose-built complex that had its own facilities, including a shop, restaurant and even a hairdressing facility.

For those of you who know Pam, she is a person who is in constant contact with God, praying about everything, however little or however big. She asked God that if she was having an apartment there, could she please have a bedroom for the extra equipment. Also, could she have a balcony as she loved the feeling of outdoor space.

Her delight when she heard she'd been granted an apartment there was slightly jaded by the fact that it had one bedroom with no balcony, but nevertheless she was very grateful. She took up her tenancy and began her life in her new environment.

The MS progressed and walking even with the FES was no longer possible. This particular day Pam began to feel very down. One of her support workers had called that day and talked with her, and had great concerns for her welfare. Within hours she returned with the manager of the complex. Much to his surprise and Pam's, after just twelve weeks they offered her another apartment with two bedrooms. Did it have a balcony that she had prayed for, you might be asking? It not only had a balcony, but two balconies! God had answered her prayers even more abundantly than she'd asked.

Pam shared that the flat was in perfect order and was so light and airy. The balconies were spacious with plenty of room for her to manoeuvre her wheelchair onto the balconies with their colourful potted plants to make them into her special garden. The extra bedroom could now be used to store the endless new equipment that was becoming necessary for her to remain independent, with carers who came in four times a day to see to her needs.

The view from her first-floor balcony was of a beautiful tree that housed many birds that would sing their hearts out as if to entertain her. As she furthered her gaze, she looked into our church forecourt and building.

Because of Pam's need for a mechanical wheelchair most of the time, she found it impossible to get into a conventional car and so she was unable to get to her own church in the city. Talks between her city pastor and the pastor of our church soon commenced and she was asked if she would like to be part of Parklands community. We would welcome her as part of our family, and love and care for her. She took up the offer and loved it from the start. A rota was set up, which lasted a year, to help get her from her flat to the church for the services.

As a church we were so enriched to have Pam as part of us. Her courage and determination, her faith and prayer life were and are an example to many.

During the next year-and-a-half the only place she could get to was Parklands Church. She held fellowship meetings and prayer meetings in her flat, but could only go out as far as the church. I mentioned earlier that a conventional car or taxi was impossible for her to get into. Being a tall and elegant lady now had the disadvantage of not allowing her the headroom to travel this way. For over eighteen months she wasn't able to go out except for her visits to our church on Sundays just yards away.

Pam had applied for an electric wheelchair and after some time it was delivered. It must have been so daunting for her as it arrived, but God had that in hand too. Mark, one of our now elders of the church, works for the NHS and part of his job was to design bespoke wheelchairs. He came alongside Pam and taught her how to use the wheelchair, and had it tailored to her needs.

It wasn't long before Pam mastered this mean machine and was bombing around Sketty enjoying her first freedom for eighteen months! Following that she plucked up the courage and began using a bus on her own. The bus drivers soon got to know her and enjoyed the banter as they popped open the ramp for her to wheel herself onto the bus. Off into the city she'd go, shopping for her needs, visiting the Marina weekly, enjoying various wheelchair-friendly cafés for social visits with her friends.

But what's all this to do with Pam's —dash? Let me tell you…

When we first met nearly seven years ago, Pam was praying for healing. We also joined her in this. We also know, but don't understand, that some people are healed and some are not. But it's still right to continue to pray for healing.

As Pam and I prayed, I had a sense that God placed a phrase strongly into my mind. I felt I wanted to share this with Pam. The phrase was 'in the meantime'. While Pam waited for God to heal her, what was she going to do 'in the meantime'? Powerful words. I left her with this thought.

She pondered it, reflected over it, was probably cross with it as it insinuated a gap, a pause, *a dash,* in between what she wanted more than anything else in the world – her healing.

She grappled with this before God and began to realise that her disabilities were growing and she was now unable to walk at all and also needing hoisting in her home for every different position.

Pam had a great burden and love for the homeless. Very soon her spare room for extra equipment began to fill with socks, gloves, hats, clothes, food and all things that those homeless people in the city would need. She would raise money, buy from the internet, receive donations – even her lounge began to fill with goodies for the homeless.

You might think she would contact an organisation to distribute all she'd collected. Not our Pam! Most Saturdays during the winter months, between her carers' visits to see to her needs, she would hop on a bus, having got her electric wheelchair fully charged for its mission, heavily-laden with necessities for our city homeless! What a woman! What a challenge for those of us who are able bodied. She often took a friend with her to help but many times would arrive in some notorious area on her own.

On one occasion Pam found herself in a comprising situation. The other homeless people could see she was in danger and surrounded her to protect her. Pam did have a rethink about her safety and after many months of doing this alone, felt it was time to join up with organisations who had the same passion and care as she had.

What an amazing way to use her —dash. Despite in these recent months only being able to move a few fingers on her left hand, as most of her body is paralysed, she continues to reach out to others. Praying daily for many many people and encouraging those who come into her path.

During lockdown 2020 and all the restrictions that were put on us, I thought Pam would be stuck in with no buses available. Not Pam; with her wheelchair fully charged, her beautiful long hair flowing in the breeze, she could be seen whizzing precariously at top speed on a sunny afternoon to do a social distancing few laps of her streets. She progressed as time moved on to the beautiful Singleton Park, enjoying the mass of vibrant flowers and many squirrels that frequented the botanical gardens.

Pam is an example to all of us. She had a choice: she could sit in her wheelchair in gloom as she waited for God to mend her body. But she chose to embrace the —dash in her life by making the most of every day. We all continue to pray for her to be healed and thank God for bringing her into our community of Parklands Church.

I'm sure Pam's story has inspired you to add more colour in your life. Whatever may have clipped your wings, it's time to look at this dash in your life to live each day to its fullest, seeing the restrictions that may be placed upon you as a springboard of opportunities.

That's what God does in our lives. We need never feel redundant in God's eyes. We have a purpose until we draw our very last breath.

The dash in our lives may be the most important thing we ever do on earth.

***

Let me share with you my —dash. My —dash has been somewhat different – Covid-19, the lockdown.

In the last chapter of my previous book, I talked briefly of my encounter with the Covid-19 lockdown of Spring 2020. Being a very cautious person, I rigidly stuck to the rules and virtually isolated myself in my haven and safe place of my Shalom4. Wonderful kind friends at church would bring me shopping I needed alongside my online big shop: such a great help in a time that was so uncertain.

The late Spring weather was beautiful, so the 'off the treadmill feel' gave a sense of holiday emotions amongst the deep sadness as we saw the unprecedented times we were in and the death toll rising as I dug in and isolated, being extra careful not to catch Covid-19.

Being a project person, I was so glad to take up the role of a sewing lady. Through friends on social media we were able to form a team of willing workers and we made hundreds of laundry bags, buttoned hairbands and bandanas for the hospice, and in turn they shared with the hospitals as they needed them too.

My lovely neighbour Ann even got involved and many days we sat in the sun sewing on hundreds of buttons as well as dozens of bandanas. We felt useful and were so glad that we could help our amazing NHS staff. When the needs were met, I found a gap in my day.

Living alone sometimes has its disadvantages and in these times that we could never have imagined we would go through, it could get a bit lonely. The internet was an essential for me – video links with my family, Zoom church meetings, chats to friends on my beloved iPad all kept me from total isolation.

As the time went to weeks and the weeks into months, I could see that those who were walking or cycling were in fact still on this Earth. I thought it was time, after nearly twelve weeks of only leaving my house to deliver an occasional dinner to my friend's doorstep just three houses from mine, to leave the safety of my boundaries to reach a nearby park with its green spaces and beautiful trees.

Equipped with my mask and antiseptic hand gel, I set off. It was wonderful to escape my restricted boundaries and enjoy the beauty of nature around me. My confidence was building over that period of seven days of walking and exploring places I had never visited.

On my fourth walk I decided to change my route and try a different one. Not far from my home I came off the pavement to socially distance from a runner who was using the pavement as a track. As I mounted the kerb I lost my footing and went sprawling onto the hard tarmac, breaking my right hand and partly tearing the hamstring to my right leg.

Having isolated for those months and finally picking up the courage to brave the masked, socially-distancing world, I was propelled into having no choice but to visit the A&E Department. The taxi driver arrived to take me to hospital. I struggled to get into the vehicle with my leg in spasm and my right hand refusing to work to do up my seatbelt. We drove off with my head hanging out of the window like the dogs do for safe fresh air, as the taxi driver coughed away unmasked.

I returned home having succumbed to Bri from my church family picking me up and taking me home. We respected the two-metre distancing and full on fresh air with every window wide open for safety. I was so grateful.

So here I was, being right-handed and living on my own; I knew it was going to be a challenge.

My sewing projects and my braving the outside world by walking were firmly halted, at least for a month or so. The first few days were very painful. Walking was difficult and I needed a crutch for safety when I went into the garden. My hand in plaster made life a little more challenging, but I must say my left hand stepped up and I was surprised what it could do.

The weather was beautifully sunny and I could just about manage to lower myself gingerly onto my sun-bed in the garden and bake myself like a stranded whale for a few hours. But I could see how I could allow myself to vegetate and develop the POM syndrome (poor old me).

I'm so grateful that God cares for us completely. He knew my project mentality and my need to be creative and useful each day. I was now minus the sewing and walking in my daily life which was likely to be for some time.

This was another DASH—

I must admit I didn't expect Him to give me such a request as to write a sequel. But here I was with time on my hands. Even as lockdown eased I couldn't walk too far and sewing was difficult until my hand healed. I knew I had to make the most of what might seem an incapacitated time to a God-given dash in my life for Him. Months went on as healing took place and I knew I could thank God for yet another 'dash' He had provided me with.

Challenge

Maybe I've got you thinking? What about me? Is there a —dash in my life? ...and if so, what am I doing about it? Am I wishing it away or am I allowing God to use this time to stop me rushing around to jump off the treadmill of life; to be still and listen to His voice again; to follow His leadings instead of my own agenda?

However difficult your dash may be, let me reassure you – it will not be wasted if you let Him into it to challenge you, change you, heal you.

What have you got to lose? Invite Him into your dash and see it supernaturally change what was maybe mundane to exciting and life-changing for ever!

Prayer

Lord Jesus, take my —dash and transform my life because of it. Give me courage to let You have Your way as I lay down this time in my life. I trust You with the outcome, knowing You only want the best for me. Thank you, Lord Jesus. Amen.

4

GOD OF THE 'BE THERE'

Two very ordinary and somewhat insignificant words; yet they can be life-changing. I wonder where you are at as you read these words.

I had just entered the second Covid-19 lockdown. The nights had begun to draw in and the chill of the autumnal air dictated that Summer was finally over and it was time to baton down the hatches and prepare for whatever the cold north winds would deliver to us. It was six months into the pandemic and life changed completely. The 'new normal' had become the way of life.

The Sunday on-line church service had ended and as the screen went blank and the worship sounds disappeared into silence, I reflected and these words filled my mind:

'My world has shrunk, shrunk to a size that I could never have imagined. It's not age or ill health that has made it so small, but the threat of Covid-19.'

I sat in my favourite seat looking out at my favourite view and marvelled at what I once used to take for granted; this had now become the highlight of my day.

The autumnal scene revealed itself as I gazed ahead, the gentle breeze catching the dancing leaves that would soon fall to reveal the bareness of the branch that carried it through the Spring and Summer. The last of the Summer sun warmed late blooms that majestically showed their beauty. The sound of the birdsong brought delight to my ears throughout these lockdown seasons.

I may had been restricted like so many but I was grateful for all that I saw before me. Oh yes, I missed my old normal, but I thank God that I could say, 'I embrace my new normal and am so truly grateful for all I have.'

For many of us, this new normal robbed us of what was once our routine our lives, our jobs, joys and passions. Adjustment didn't come overnight, but we got there. We had to embrace this new way of doing life otherwise we risked losing heart, and even the will to go on if we lost hope.

If, like me, you have retired from your workplace and have filled your life volunteering or with the things on your 'to do' bucket list, you may well have felt somewhat adrift with the restrictions placed upon us for the first time in our lives because of the pandemic.

So what has all this to do with the chapter heading of 'God of the Be There'?

We can shuffle the words around and for many of us can confidently say God will 'be there' for us through these trials and stormy times. And He will. But taking the sentence in context, we too can **be there** for those who need us. Never underestimate the role and job description of simply being a 'be there'. It has the power to change lives.

***

Here's Jan's story:

In the last weeks of her life, my lovely mum Beth, who had Alzheimer's, astounded everyone in the lounge of the wonderful Hengoed Parc Care Home. I had asked if they had a keyboard to see if, as a pianist, she could remember how to play anything, having not played for months.

Mum showed no recognition of the keyboard as I held it in front of her, and didn't even really appear to be able to see it (also having macular degeneration). I placed her hands on the keyboard, and she proceeded to play a virtually perfect rendition of 'What a Friend We Have in Jesus'! Such a beautiful and emotional moment!

A couple of years later, I had been struggling personally for some time, due to a stock-pile of grief and various other life stressors. At a time when maintaining friendships was hard enough due to the Covid-19 pandemic, another 'Beth' reached out the hand of friendship to me in a really profound way.

We were previously acquainted through the wonders of the church community, but we didn't know each other at all well. Beth did not allow this to deter her, so at a time when I really needed a friend, she committed to consistently 'being there' for me. She was warm, kind and generous with her time and energy.

I do not doubt that Beth was responding to the divine prompting of our Heavenly Father, who had compassion on me and sent her to me, like an angel of the morning to herald in a 'new dawn', as I transitioned into a new 'chapter' of life.

I liken this to the story of my mum, because Beth's undeterred determination to reach me with her joyful, honest, non-demanding friendship at that time, came as the very 'hands and feet' of Jesus, as it were. In reality this was more of a video link 'voice and smile' of Jesus, as we were unable to meet up.

Beth did however engage her creative hands in making me lovely personal, home-made gifts.

As a faithful representative and sincere follower of Jesus, Beth beautifully demonstrated to me the authenticity of that age-old truth – what a friend we have in Jesus. Hallelujah!

***

Being available as a ‘be there’ is a precious ministry. Simply being there for people can change the course of their lives. The privilege of standing in the gap, taking time to listen without judging, offering compassion and kindness, can save a life spiritually, emotionally and sometimes physically, helping through what could be the hardest times in their lives.

Does that mean we feel full of wisdom and advice? Certainly not! Actually we often feel inadequate and wonder why they are turning to us for help. The good news is that when God sends, He equips. As we take time to be still and listen with His heart, we know His leading to walk alongside and journey through with these souls as it ‘comes to pass’, as the King James Bible so often quotes in its books.

I was reminded recently by a lovely young lady that I have the privilege of being a ‘be there’. She asked me to write about the importance of being a ‘be there’.

Simply just doing that. Journeying through the joys and sorrows, holding in there with them, believing in them, listening intently, being willing to offer advice when asked, having the courage to lovingly challenge if necessary. The result is that we take the love, acceptance and compassion of Jesus to them in their times of need. Is there anything more worthwhile?

So, as we use these times of apparent inactivity to our old normal, they can in fact be the very tool to take us into a new realm of loving and caring.

I asked a dear friend what a 'be there' meant to that friend: '*Being there* is a tangible, though sometimes silent, supportive presence. An assurance of commitment to companionship, no matter how rocky your road, or how many times you may stumble or fall; no pressure to please or perform; a sincere and generously available friend.' JM

Challenge

Could I be a 'be there' in more ways than I've ever been before? It may be costly. There probably will be a sacrifice of your time and energy. The rewards, however, outnumber all the hours you spend loving and giving. God loves a... ***be there****...*

Prayer

Lord, I offer myself afresh to You to be a 'be there' for the hurting and the lost in new ways. Please use me to bring love and compassion to those You send to me to show the love and acceptance that You have given me. Thank you, Lord Jesus. Amen.

5

GOD OF THE GUEST BOOK

Have you ever been tempted to have a guest book? Nearly nine years ago I opened my home to be a place for weary ladies to rest a while, be refreshed and restored, ministered to and able to get back out there to continue the journey in their lives.

I decided that a guest book would be a good idea. Maybe you think it's a bit presumptuous to have a book displayed for guests to write their comments about their visit or stay in your home. It can be a source of encouragement to you and many as the comments are read and re-read over the months and years.

Sometimes their comments help you tweak the way you present things or give you ideas on how to improve on your hospitality. All good stuff when you seek to serve the Lord by sharing your home, time and love with those He sends to your haven.

I thought it would be a nice idea to introduce some of the guests who have come through the doors of Shalom4, especially at this time when the house has been void of visitors because of Covid restrictions making hospitality forbidden and the very passion of my heart being made impotent.

Many of you who read my first book will know that following my father's death I used my inheritance to update the house I now live in to make it a place where

I could invite weary ladies to rest and stay awhile as they received TLC, got recharged and reinvigorated to go back out there able to face the world again, refreshed and energised.

When God challenged me to write this sequel and before I went into major panic mode, I heard him whisper, 'Draw from your memories.'

My guest book contains the memories of those who paused on their journeys for a while and got restored by God here at Shalom4. Some names have been changed to protect their anonymity. Let's open the book together.

It's a damp, late November day and I've lit the fire so you may be warmed and I invite you to sit on one of my comfy chairs. Recline if you like, the sound of the crackle of the logs burning brightly on the log burner, shedding its warmth in the room. I wrap a soft blanket around your legs. A steaming hot chocolate, or a coffee if you'd prefer, or even a choice of many fruit teas. Grab one of my soft cushions, cwtching* you into a restful pose to listen to their stories. (*the word 'cwtch' is a Welsh word for a very safe, appropriate, special cuddle or hug.)

Are you sitting comfortably?… then I'll begin…

As I open the book some thank-you cards fall out onto my lap. I read them, recalling the precious souls that have sent a thankful card for their stay at Shalom4.

I remember the preparations I have made before their visit: praying for them, catering for their individual needs, the bright guest room refreshed and sparkling; a vase of colourful flowers especially bought for them, a welcome card placed on neatly-folded, freshly-laundered towels with a pamper bottle of lotion tucked in them ready on their bed.

Lara

Let me introduce you to Lara. Lara I knew from many years ago. She was a bubbly Pentecostal Christian who suffered for many years with a condition that affected her kidneys, making her permanently unwell and in kidney failure. Yet she never grumbled. Lara was of petite frame remaining neatly and beautifully dressed. Lara loved the Lord and was always full of praise for her Saviour. Such was the reality of her faith in Jesus.

Lara had cancer. She longed to be healed. It was a huge blow when she had a further diagnosis of terminal cancer on top of her liver condition; yet her faith never wavered.

As she battled in the months to come, it was more apparent that palliative treatment was the only way forward. One of her friends approached me with the possibility of Lara coming to stay at Shalom4 for some well-needed respite. I was delighted to invite her with open arms, but knew my limitations. So it was with trepidation that I opened the door to her on a cold December day.

Lara was a shadow of her former self. The cancer had ravaged her body which had been reduced to skin and bone. I took her luggage and helped her settle into the guest room for her stay. I sat her in the recliner chair in the lounge so that she had a good view and plenty of light. I wrapped her in a soft warm blanket as she acclimatised to her place of retreat for the next four days.

Because eating had become a problem, she was nervous to be away from home. I quickly put her mind at rest as she learnt how I lived on a very restricted diet and could accommodate her diet very easily.

As she settled into the TLC of Shalom4, she began to share with me that she wasn't afraid of dying, but the process of it. I was able to reassure her of hospice involvement if and when it would be needed.

I soon became aware of how much effort it had taken for her to come to me for this period of respite and wanted her to get everything that God had for her while she was here. Lara faced her Heaven-bound journey with such courage and in total reality. She was not angry with God for not healing her but now accepted that her total healing would happen when she had left this Earth for Heaven.

We talked much; she grieved, cried, laughed and even had joy in those few precious days we had together. She wrote some lovely words in the guest book about her stay at Shalom4. Her highlight, as she wrote in the book and typical of the person she was, was on the Wednesday evening when she decided she would love to have a bath. I knew she was very weak so I wasn't sure if this was a good idea, but it's something she longed for.

I kept my ear pealed and sure enough about ten minutes into her bath time I heard her weak voice cry out to me with a giggle in the tone, 'Sue, I'm stuck, I can't get out!' I rushed up, grabbing some extra towels to preserve her dignity and gently got her on her knees. She was so tiny and emancipated that I soon managed to scoop her up into a safe place. She emerged wrapped warmly in towel and just laughed and laughed. What a woman!

As her stay came to an end, she felt calm and peaceful, loved and focused, recharged and able to face the necessary putting things in order as she wanted to leave this Earth having done all this. What a privilege it was to serve her during these few days.

A little excerpt from her entry in the guest book: 'I'm finding it hard to put pen to paper what this rest and respite has meant. It's such a God-given gift as we are set aside to rest. We've had times of sharing, I may have grief or some tears – this place is a special place – an oasis money cannot buy, with peace and tender loving care…'

Thirty-six days later Lara left for Heaven, having got all she wanted done and ready to meet her Saviour Jesus in Heaven where there would be no more pain or suffering. Rest in peace, dear 'Lara'.

***

Dawn

My dear friend Dawn whom I wrote about in my first book also has entries in my guest book. Dawn continues to serve me with her artistic and talented gifting in designing the covers of my books with Diyan Kantardgiev, a very talented photographer videographer.

Dawn and I have been friends for over two decades. We met at church and have always remained really close friends. I shared previously how she discovered she had a breast lump just as she and I were launching her first craft show. We were exuberant and brimming with excitement as we planned the practicalities of the stall to sell her pictures. Then she dropped the bombshell as we talked just days before the event that she had found a breast lump.

I urged her to visit her doctor. She did this and within a very short time she was in the loop of visits to the Breast Care Unit and all that follows with the diagnosis of stage 2 breast cancer.

Very soon she started treatment and the effects of radiotherapy and chemotherapy took their toll. The tiredness that can only be described by fellow patients is nothing short of being completely wiped out; 'flu doesn't come near the awful feeling.

After completing one cycle of treatment, Dawn decided that she would like to try out Shalom4 and have some respite. This actually was right at the beginning of the opening of Shalom4. Dawn was my 'guinea pig' to try out and help me change anything that wasn't quite suitable. I still had finishing touches to do. It was such a privilege to have her. One thing God had impressed on me was to tailor-make each person's stay.

For Dawn the first few days were essential for sleep and more sleep. She loved the memory foam mattress and the comfort it brought. Her own en-suite gave her privacy and of course the TLC that Shalom4 offered without measure.

Dawn stayed a few times as she proceeded with her treatment. We had some lovely times together as she strengthened and healed over the months, A couple of lines from her second entry in the guest book:

'Had a great time with Caz (a friend) and Sue, plenty of laughter therapy. Came for peace and quiet to the dulcet tones of the pneumatic drill! (*oops, sorry Dawn*)…Sue's got me working on a butterfly mosaic, she doesn't like to see idle hands….' 2013

Dawn continues to go from strength to strength. Her work has taken her far beyond the first craft show we did together those years ago.

She is a breast cancer survivor. Check out her website to find out more about her and her beautiful artwork. She can be contacted at **www.koinoniastudio.art**.

***

Anna

Anna has been a friend of mine for years. She and her husband have a busy life in South East England. Anna is a quirky, fun-loving, colourful person who has been through much in her life. We share the same year of birth so we were both bulge babies post Second World War.

Over the years she has literally dropped into my home often in bits, at the end of her tether, exhausted and with major crises in her life and the lives around her. I love it that she feels she can gain by just spending time together.

I loved one of her entries in my guest book:

'This weary soul arrived feeling almost hopeless. Four days later I feel alive, contented, full of hope and excitement for what God has planned for my life. I am so so grateful…'

Yet again God has been faithful to His word. He alone does the healing and loving. All He asks of me is to be available and open to all those He sends. What a privilege it is to serve Him this way.

It's such an encouragement to me as I finger through the entries and draw from my memories as I read through.

***

Jen

Jen came to me as a stranger. She had been in need of rest. A friend of hers had been told of this cosy little home in Swansea that offered respite for weary ladies, and she contacted me. This was a bit scary for me as up to that point I had ladies I knew staying with me, so this was a first.

I prayed that my home Shalom4 and I would be what this young lady needed and that God would meet her every need. And He did… From her entry in the guest book:

'Absolutely does beyond what is says on the label. Overwhelmed, overjoyed and so so grateful. Exceedingly abundantly beyond all I ever could have asked or hoped for. Arrived a weary, dusty, down-trodden traveller and found an oasis of love, care, provision, kindness, friendship, wonderful conversations and home-cooked food. God really showed up...more in fact than ever seen before. I feel strengthened, uplifted, refreshed and delighted...my heart is bursting with love and appreciation…'

***

Before I come to a close, I cannot finish this guest book chapter without mentioning Em.

Since beginning this ministry, I had strong convictions that Shalom4 was a short-term respite for many reasons. So when I was approached by a lovely young trainee doctor in our church who desperately needed accommodation, I felt I needed to make an exception. Em was in her final crucial year before becoming a qualified doctor. She needed a place of peace where she could feel safe and loved. This would help her studies which was paramount.

Em arrived to a room with bunting and welcome cards and immediately settled in. We had agreed it would be a bit like student living and she would have the freedom to cook her own meals and come and go as she pleased. This fitted in with both our lifestyles and worked out so well. I did enjoy being Mama Sue to her and cooking the occasional meals for her. It was such a great time for me too: many laughs, sharing times, aromas of cooking and baking as Em displayed her culinary skills.

Her romance blossomed and she became betrothed to Jamie. Em qualified as a doctor and I had the absolute delight of having her stay the night before her wedding too. What a privilege! They are a family now and have a beautiful little girl called Florence. How wonderful to have all these memories of when Shalom4 blessed them.

***

As I re-read these words in the book it reminds me of God's faithfulness to His promise and what He simply asked me to do – open my home to weary ladies. Simply that. To give them TLC. To take them to the feet of Jesus for Him to do all the healing necessary. To leave Shalom4, able to be refreshed and carry on their journey in their life.

I feel particularly sad that so much has been robbed at this time because of Covid-19 restrictions. But I cannot afford to stay in that train of thought. We need to hand the ministry that He has lent us back to Him so that He can refashion them into a new shape so that He can use us from our homes even with the strictest restrictions in place. He is able to do this if we are prepared to let go and let Him have His way.

I put on social media that I celebrated the years of having a sign 'Room at the Inn' over my door. A dear friend, Julie Johnson, put this on my social media page that sums up Shalom4:

A place of welcome
A place of peace
A place of healing
A place to meet.
A place of laughter
A place where tears are replaced with joy

A place of safety where one can lie
Cakes and sandwiches in abundance
Music and testimony, prayers for the lost
A place that God ordained and filled with His love
Blessed by His Spirit and grace from above
Even in times where we cannot meet
Sue with her smile is there to greet
A kindly word, spoken in season
A lavender heat bag or cushion for phone
All can be lovingly provided at this home
So bless you Sue for this safe haven.

How very very precious to receive this and know that it is all of God! His love and grace, His ministry…

Challenge

Are you willing to step out of the boat into the ministry God has given you? Perhaps it's become mundane and joyless especially with the restrictions of Covid-19. Are you and I willing to embrace our ministry that might not look like its past shape, and as we face a new normal, handing it back to God to allow Him to remould us to be even more effective in the ministry gifting he has lent us?

Prayer

Lord Jesus, I give You back the ministry You entrusted into my hands. There is no safer place for it to be. Place back into my hands the things You would have me do in my new normal... Lord, I am willing. Amen

6
GOD OF THE ABSTINENCE

I shared this little story with a friend who hooted with laughter as I unfolded how God had challenged me with this abstinence.

Let me tell you...

Alcohol. To most teenagers, in the days when I was growing up, alcohol was attractive and we couldn't wait till we were eighteen to start legally experimenting with it. In those days we hardly heard about drugs and it certainly wasn't something I would get into with my lifestyle of church, the Girl Guide movement and all that went with it.

But with alcohol it seemed different. Smoking was so common and my parents smoked every day, so we were brought up in that environment. I was told as a teenager that they couldn't stop me smoking but I was to buy my own cigarettes. To be honest as young teenagers my sister and I tried rolling tea leaves to smoke. That cured us for life! It was an unforgettable experience that helped us both make a decision that we would never smoke.

But alcohol had its own attractions. It was so socially accepted and expected that when you were eighteen you would start going into pubs and enjoy alcoholic drinks. Two glasses of sherry or wine and that lovely relaxed feeling would begin, everything seemed funny and chilled and of course we were part of an 'in' crowd.

In those days to ask for a non-alcoholic drink at a bar was seen to be somewhat weird. This was before the days of the drink-driving ban. To ask for a coffee or tea would have been totally unheard of, and if you'd asked for tap water, well you probably would have been thrown out!

I liked that relaxed feeling that alcohol first gave me, although I remember my first time drinking gin and spent the rest of the evening crying with depression. Then there was the next morning. The ghastly feeling in my head and stomach and a strong decision of never again! But I always did! I found decorating a room so much easier with a bottle of Cinzano to aid me along.

I could take it or leave it, so I have God to thank that it never gripped me to the point of dependency.

During the weeks back in the 1980s when God was calling me to commit my life to Him, I remember this day that changed everything.

It was the wedding of Charles and Diana. A few friends had decided to meet at a local pub to celebrate. The owner of the pub decided to offer champagne to us all and then everyone continued with their own drinks.

It was a very hot day. We walked to the pub to meet our friends. I had never found it very stimulating sitting for hours in this environment but I was a crowd-follower and didn't want to be the odd one out.

The men in the group passed by their champagne as they were mostly beer and cider drinkers. So I was given their champagne. Most of you will probably know that it's very pleasant to drink.

The heat was unbearable in this pub so I began drinking the free champagne lined up for me like it was apple juice. An hour later I went to get up and…wow…I could hardly stand! Then it was time to go. I staggered to my feet and was horrified to find I wasn't in control of my legs! Being the Brown Owl of the area, I was horrified at the thought of losing my reputation of being a good, upright and responsible citizen.

We walked along the pavement that joined the church walkway and as I got to the steps to join the rest of the pavement, I went flying! My leg from below my knee down along the shin bone was badly cut. I was so thankful I had on a long skirt covering the evidence of my drunken fall.

I refused to continue to go up the steep public road and insisted that I took the woods walk home, which you can imagine was much harder. However, my self-righteousness was protected as no one could see me. I got home, limping badly, and managed to bathe my bleeding, hurting leg and attempted to sober up. I must say it was a horrible evening, but it taught me a great lesson!

This all happened during the time when God was moving in my life. I knew this wasn't the way for me any more. That day I vowed to the Lord that I would never drink alcohol again. Even then I could see that it could have easily become a dependency for me in the hard times ahead. But my vow to Him has stuck firm to this day and I have no need for alcohol at all, as the joy I feel inside doesn't depend on a quick fix and substance. It's supernatural God-given joy.

Hallelujah!

Sadly, years later alcohol was to become the very thing that ruined my marriage and I could see God's care and love by bringing me to the place of being teetotal. This really helped me to be involved in a small way by supporting Teen Challenge, a Christian organisation helping those who had become substance-dependent to come off drugs and drink that had ruined their lives. I do not judge anyone who enjoys to drink alcohol, but I do know first-hand how quickly that social drink can lead to addiction and ruin lives, even leading to death.

So I thank God for allowing me to fall down those church steps those years ago. It saved me from ending up in the disaster of dependency. I have no doubt that His ways are beyond our understanding, and always for our best.

Let me finish this chapter by sharing something else I have abstinence from – coffee. Many years ago when we, as a group of friends, were praying together, I was praying for a family member who was alcohol-dependent. Suddenly a wise and discerning Christian man stopped me, saying God was challenging me about my dependency/addiction. I was indignant! I hadn't got one, but he insisted I had.

As we prayed further, the Holy Spirit revealed to me that it was coffee! I would drink over twenty cups a day! It had become a habit. I just loved my coffee. But that day I decided I would wean myself off it and drink decaf only. I can tell you it was hard! It took me over a month for the cravings and headaches to go.

Eventually I settled on decaf coffee until some years after I made another vow to support a young friend who had gone through the Teen Challenge programme. I would give up coffee altogether as a vow and belief in her never going back on alcohol. Two decades on and our abstinence vows are as strong as the day we made them.

We have a God of the impossible. Hallelujah!

Challenge

As you read this chapter you may have identified with something I said about dependency, or addiction. Can I say if you did, then God wants to show you the way out to set you free. Maybe it's not for you but a loved one; then pray for that person to be set free.

Prayer

Lord Jesus, I need Your help to break free from the dependency that threatens my life. I invite You into this area of my life that has a hold on me. Please lead me out into Your freedom. Thank you for loving and caring for me by convicting me of all that puts me in chains. Amen.

7
GOD OF THE TEARS

The most welcome sound that a new parent and midwife will hear is that of the cry of a newborn baby. The relief is tangible as the baby begins to take in oxygen and a lusty cry echoes through the walls of the delivery suite. I'm sure baby isn't too thrilled to have made the journey from the comfort of a safe place in mother's womb, into the narrow birth canal and then yanked out into bright lights and a strange new world. No wonder baby cries!

But have you ever noticed there are no tears. This will take a couple of weeks to happen. I've learned today that in fact the tear ducts don't actually make the tears but they are made by the lacrimal glands. By the time the newborn is three months old, the tears should be flowing. We know babies cry if they are hungry, in pain and uncomfortable. Crying highlights comfort and care.

But what about us? As a child, I remember the first time I cried tears of pain and emotion was when my beloved cat, Timmy, died. I cried buckets with sadness. Tears seemed easy at that age. I would feel an emotion or be in distress and I would simply cry.

So we take for granted that when we're sad, in pain or distressed in any way, we will cry. But that's not always the case. For me my tears dried up through a traumatic time in my first marriage. I was locked in a time for two years of not being able to feel heat or the cold – emotions were non-existent.

Sometimes a person will tell about a deep sadness rising up the chest and into the throat, almost willing the tears to come, but they were stuck. No release for them, swallowing the heaviness down and feeling even more ghastly.

I remember my dear mum saying that she couldn't cry and found it so hard. However much she tried to make herself feel sad, the tears just refused to come. I think the well dried up during the time of losing her parents.

For me it was decades without the release of tears even after trauma of the time settled. I prayed for many years that I would cry again. I was stuck in a cycle that as loss after loss became my experience, I began to develop a coping strategy. This wasn't something I had made a plan for but I found that I began to get so used to the feeling of loss and it didn't seem to faze me. I longed for the release in tears. I prayed and prayed for them. I read books that helped me understand the complexity of emotions and the effects that trauma had on the individuals who suffered this way. God heard a lot of prayers over many years from me and it was years of healing that released the sea of tears that had built up inside me.

I began to find my feelings and emotions leave the time warp that they had for so long learnt to malfunction in. I remember the surprise when I felt a strong emotion and the result was a warm watery feeling coming from my eyes which ran down my cheeks with a salty taste as it passed across my lips, landing on my chest and forming a damp patch on my T-shirt. At first I was afraid to move in case it stopped. The sheer relief that after all this time I could still cry was mind-blowing to me. I felt normal again. The sense of release was tangible. I knew a healing had taken place and I was now reconnected with no time lapse between the emotion and the tears that followed.

My tears were shed in joy as well as in grief or sorrow. I was moved by music, memories, compassion and empathy, to name but a few that brought me to tears.

Some years ago during a training session in the hospice, we were told something I found quite profound about tears. When we produce tears through peeling an onion, if those tears are analysed, they are simply water. When we produce tears through sadness or pain, these tears may look like a pool of water formed by our crying, but they are in fact different. They contain chemicals that if not released have toxins in and can cause depression unless released from the body.

When we have one of those times of sobbing from the core of our being and the tears are bouncing off us, we feel absolutely worn out and tired. It has been proved at this stage that we produce a substance which is a natural sedative that calms us and makes us feel sleepy, giving us time to rest the body and mind after such a release.

Isn't God so clever! I have to add something I

mentioned in my first book about laughter therapy. When we laugh, that belly-shaking type laugh that produces tears, we actually produce endorphins that give us a sense of well-being. Fascinating stuff, isn't it?

Are you stuck? Have past hurts caused you to put your guard up from your emotions? Are you frightened to cry because you think once you release those floodgates, they will never stop?

Well, I've got good news for you. God has it and is in control. You are safe to let go and trust Him with everything. It is part of your healing, like it was mine; done in His time at the pace He knows you can cope with. He will never overwhelm you, so great is His love.

Challenge

Do you feel it's time to give Him those hidden scars, those tears that are deep within the core of your being, locked up for fear that you will never be able to face them again? Rest assured that He has His arms outstretched, longing for you to let Him bathe and heal your wounds.

Prayer

Lord Jesus, I long to be set free from all the pains that have scarred and damaged me in the past. I give You permission to begin a new healing work in my heart to restore me and make me whole once again. I know I am safe in Your arms. Please open up the pain in my heart and release the tears to flow. Amen.

8

GOD OF THE PRODIGAL

The Story of the Lost Son: Luke 15:11-22 (The Message)

11–12 Then he said, 'There was once a man who had two sons. The younger said to his father, "Father, I want right now what's coming to me."

12–16 'So the father divided the property between them. It wasn't long before the younger son packed his bags and left for a distant country. There, undisciplined and dissipated, he wasted everything he had. After he had gone through all his money, there was a bad famine all through that country and he began to hurt. He signed on with a citizen there who assigned him to his fields to slop the pigs. He was so hungry he would have eaten the corncobs in the pig slop, but no one would give him any.

17–20 'That brought him to his senses. He said, "All those farmhands working for my father sit down to three meals a day, and here I am starving to death. I'm going back to my father. I'll say to him, Father, I've sinned against God, I've sinned before you; I don't deserve to be called your son. Take me on as a hired hand." He got right up and went home to his father.

20–21 'When he was still a long way off, his father saw him. His heart pounding, he ran out, embraced him, and kissed him. The son started his speech:

"Father, I've sinned against God, I've sinned before you; I don't deserve to be called your son ever again."

22–24 'But the father wasn't listening. He was calling to the servants, "Quick. Bring a clean set of clothes and dress him. Put the family ring on his finger and sandals on his feet. Then get a grain-fed heifer and roast it. We're going to feast! We're going to have a wonderful time! My son is here given up for dead and now alive! Given up for lost and now found!" And they began to have a wonderful time.'

If you're anything like me, this is one of the parables and stories that as a child I loved. My imagination could vividly conjure this story of restoration. The story clearly depicts the separation and pain that this father felt when his younger son left the safety of the fold to go out into the world to taste of its fruits as he squandered his inheritance. Having hit rock bottom and seen the errors of his way, he had no place to go except to return to his father for forgiveness for his rebellious ways.

Did his father lecture him, beat him, make him feel unworthy and the bottom of the pile? No…he saw him coming along the path, got the best of everything ready for him – clothes, a feast – and they ran into each other's arms, embracing, marvelling, filled with great joy to be reunited with each other.

Each one of us before we turned our lives to Jesus did exactly the same; we went our own way. Sometimes through success, sometimes through disaster, but always through a path that caused us to be separated from our loving Heavenly Father.

Let me tell you about Judith's story.

I met Judith at church in the late 1980s. I could tell from her accent that she wasn't from the UK. She had short, greying hair and had a style that was fitting for the hippy scene. Judith was a strong, free spirit with determination that would move a mountain. She was committed to God and to values of community and fellowshipping with other believers.

Judith's passion and desire was to help those young people in Europe who were suffering from what had been front-line news during these years – AIDS. Despite having a young family and being a single mum, she juggled her commitments at home and travelled overseas on numerous occasions in mission work in Europe.

Judith had come through turbulent times and was part of the scene where substance abuse had once been part of her life. Who better to walk alongside these young people who were shunned by society and seen as modern-day lepers.

The first young man who travelled from Spain to Swansea to be loved and cared for by the fellowship and Judith's family was 'Gabe'.

Gabe was a small-framed, smiley Spanish young man who'd lost an arm and was HIV-positive. He spoke little English but managed to get himself understood. I loved to hear him giggle, but mostly I loved to hear him pray in Spanish. Even though I couldn't understand a word, I seemed to get what he was saying. Sadly his health deteriorated and he died here in Swansea. Another young Spanish man had joined the fellowship – his name was 'Alb'. Judith also helped him.

Judith decided that she would relocate to Spain and spent fifteen years there before returning to the UK. She had begun to lose focus on God, and the subtlety of our enemy enticed her away. Even though she had walked away from God, He had never left her.

So often in our lives we choose our own paths. Having known the ways of God, we too can get drawn into another way of life that doesn't include Him. We go our own way. As the song says, 'I did it my way'.

Yet that still small voice begins to get our attention. It may be just a whisper to start, but it becomes stronger. For Judith, that whisper calling her back into the safety of the fold surprisingly took her through paths of other religions and New Age teachings as she searched and searched to find the truth.

We have a God of grace who allows us to sometimes go where angels fear to tread in order for us to get back to Him. Our logic can't fathom why, but He has His reasons and one day we will have it all revealed to us. We cannot see His master plan for our lives...we see only in part.

After years of not seeing Judith, I began bumping into her. We shared the occasional bus journey together and found we had a mutual interest in photography, especially shots of flowers, and for her she loved insects and took incredible shots of them. I felt that the 'God talk' wasn't right, so we kept it light and on our mutual interest of photography. We enrolled on a course together. I actually didn't get past a few sessions because of a scheduled operation. Judith not only finished the course but had beautiful pictures that impressed so much that she was asked to exhibit them.

To get the pictures printed and mounted, Judith set out on the bus, her usual mode of transport into town to prepare the prints. She hadn't gone far when she felt very unwell, so much so that she asked a stranger, a girl also on the bus, if she would get off with her as she felt so ill.

As soon as they got off the bus Judith had a heart attack and was taken to hospital in a friend's car. When she arrived they were told had she waited for an ambulance she probably wouldn't have made it. In fact, the family were called in twice as her life dangled by a thread. Emergency surgery followed and Judith came through.

The prodigal had returned to her Father. He had waited for her...walked unseen with her through years of precarious pathways...but kept her…for such a time as this…she was redeemed, restored, forgiven and complete in Him.

Judith slowly recovered. Her heart surgery had worked and there began her deeper-than-ever-before walk with God. She knew she had been brought back from the brink of death and that it wasn't her time to leave this planet. God had plans for her before taking her to Himself.

Despite ongoing family demands that can sometimes be overwhelming, Judith throws herself upon God, trusting Him completely. She may sometimes battle with not understanding His plans or even purposes, but Judith never fails to come through, abandoning herself to His path for herself and her family.

The path isn't easy, but she can testify to the truth from scripture:

Never will I leave you; never will I forsake you. (Hebrews 13:5 NIV)

To sum up, the Judith that we see now is echoed in this quote from Proverbs 27:17: *'iron sharpens iron'*. Questioning, encouraging, coaching, challenging, with what purpose? To bring you and her nearer to the heart of God.

Quote:

It is not enough to be a useful tool for God. You must sit still for the grinding that produces the edge. (Anon)

Challenge:

Are you ready for God to sharpen you to become more the instrument or weapon He wants you to be?

Prayer:

Lord Jesus, I am willing to sit still for as long as it takes for You to produce the edge that comes from your grinding. Refine me, Lord, for your purposes. Purge the dross that causes imperfections in me. Let me come forth as gold. I give You all the glory, Lord. Amen.

Postscript…

Just over a year ago Judith felt the Lord wanted to fan

the creative gift He had given her in art. She began to paint, but her lovely bijou cottage had very little room and her worktops were full, so we arranged for her to have a table that folded down for more room. Soon even that became full. Her mind worked overtime as she thought of a way to have a place to create all that was unfolding in her mind.

The plan eventually hatched that a garden studio was the way forward. With no budget for it but lots of prayer, faith and vision, it came to pass. The funds, materials, man- and woman-power came into being and the most lovely studio was created. Her vision and dream had come true! Her artwork and creations are amazing and she can be contacted on frenkelscreativeart@gmail.com. God knew when He gave Judith her life back that she had a future and a hope…the prodigal fully restored.

9

GOD IN THE DARK PLACES

And I will give you treasures hidden in the darkness – secret riches. I will do this so you may know that I am the LORD, the God of Israel, the one who calls you by name. (Isaiah 45:3 NLT)

I start this chapter with a somewhat shaky hand. God in the dark places. If you are anything like me when I first read this scripture I wondered if I'd read it correctly. Treasures hidden in the darkness? Maybe the translation wasn't accurate. Surely treasure couldn't be found in dark places. I searched through many different Bible translations and each one came up with the same meaning. It means 'treasures in darkness'.

I'm sure there are many amazing writers who have written wonderfully on this passage, far better than I can ever do, yet I feel led to let God bring something from what I share with you. As I reflected silently, a picture in my mind's eye began to form. Darkness gave me a feeling of coldness, emptiness, rejection, abandonment – all causing great suffering at the time.

I stilled my mind on the word 'suffering'. No matter who we are in this world, sooner or later suffering will come; it's inevitable. We can shun it, run or hide from it, but it has a habit of catching up with us in the end. As I think of the times that were like being thrown in a pit and let in no light, none of us can honestly say we embrace suffering. Surely the pain of suffering is an enemy to us? If we saw Jesus standing in front of us offering us a gift and the gift was suffering, our response would be…thanks, but no thanks!

But when the darkness comes and threatens to close in on us, suffocating us like a smoke-filled room causing us to gasp frantically for air, our first response is often, 'Why is this happening to me, God; where are You in this chasm of blackness in my life?'

We join with David, who so often expressed clearly in the psalms, when he cries out in Psalm 13 – *How long, O Lord? Will you forget me forever? How long will you hide your face from me?* We can echo our prayers with David as we struggle for air to express our pain and fear in the darkness.

Sadly some have entered the Christian faith believing that when we come to Jesus we will live happily ever after. Sorry if I'm about to burst your bubble, but that simply is not true. What we do know is that Jesus will be with us every step of way.

But let's go back to the word 'suffering'. Here are a few words to describe suffering: pain, grief, distress, agony, misery, ordeal, discomfort, despair, torment, hardship, anguish, affliction, to name but a few. All these bring us into darkness. Darkness also conjures up unhealthy places, seedy even, and yet this passage clearly shows us that we can find treasures even there. How can this be? We see God as a God of light.

In the next few chapters, I want to share with you the very precious accounts of three individual families. Their stories are during the darkest, heartbreaking and most vulnerable times of their lives, yet they allowed God to come into the centre of their pain and grief. I feel very privileged that they have allowed me to include their stories in my book.

To give them the dignity and sensitivity their stories deserve, I have asked them to tell their story and experience in their own heartfelt words.

10

PAUL-JOHN'S STORY

March 4th, 1998 started like any other day, with our family going off to school and work, but before the end of the day, our lives were changed forever.

Paul-John was then our youngest of five children. He bubbled with life, was always smiling, funny, engaging, and had the ability to communicate with anyone of any age. Paul-John was sensitive to other people's needs, and in school he would befriend those who were bullied and anyone who needed a friend. His friends have said, Paul-John was a good, reliable friend to have.

Paul-John looked forward to the future! He was looking forward to embracing puberty, and would often measure his hands (palms together) against mine, to check how fast he was growing.

We had open conversations about anything and everything. Having been brought up in a larger than 'normal' family, I asked him one day how many children he would like in the future. With a glint in his eye, and a big smile, he replied 'loads'!

Paul-John was inquisitive about a lot of things, which led him to be 'busy'. For example, he would always accompany Gareth to pick me up from work at Morriston Hospital, where they waited outside the ward where I worked. There was always machinery in the corridor, and he was always asking questions about how they worked. Gareth would often ask him not to touch them, as he would be itching to press a button to try them out. (Some machines were plugged into sockets along the corridor walls in order for their batteries to recharge.)

I had recently come back to the Lord, having drifted away due to difficult circumstances in my life. After five lonesome weary years, I realised how empty my life had become. I had become bitter, cynical and angry, and didn't so much blame God, but certainly His people.

After many months of the Lord calling me back in relationship with Him, I knew how much I needed Him. In February 1998, I made the absolute right decision to go back to church, and put things right with people. It felt like going home, as I was not only welcomed by the Lord, but by His beautiful people.

Paul-John took an instant interest in my renewed faith. He was to become a teenager in the following April, so five of his years of not being in church had been a large chunk of his life. Paul-John was full of questions about God, faith, etc., which of course I loved to answer. Each day after school he would ask me if God had spoken to me that day, and would want to know what He had said.

During these days, Paul-John witnessed amazing answers to prayer. One was immediate; as I was telling him what I had prayed for that day, the phone rang, and the answer came. Paul-John was blown away.

During the last week of February, a Christian couple, friends of ours, had called around as they usually did. The wife and I went to the kitchen to make tea and coffee. Paul-John came into the kitchen and began talking about his confusion regarding having RE lessons at school, yet evolution was also taught during science lessons. I can remember speaking to Paul-John; I asked him if they had been designed and made or if they just appeared. He laughed and 'got it'. We continued in conversation, and he asked 'How can I become a Christian?' I simply explained to him, and he left the room.

Ten minutes later, Paul-John returned to the kitchen where my friend and I still were, and he said, 'I did that!' The following Sunday Paul-John came to church with me. I was overjoyed, and Mick Walford, the Pastor, welcomed him from the front.

Paul-John came home from school as usual on March 4th, but little did we know it would be for the last time.

He was OK, but there had been an incident in previous days when someone had taken his school bag, and he had found it in a puddle in the school yard. He didn't know who had done this but it had disturbed him somewhat. He was meant to go out that evening but he had a sore shoulder and the activity he engaged in was not compatible with the injury he had. He decided for the first time ever to stay home.

Earlier that evening, Paul-John went to the local shop and had bought me chocolates for my birthday for the following day. Gareth had previously told Rachel (our then youngest daughter) and Paul-John that he would take them to buy me birthday cards later in the evening.

During the evening, our older sons talked about a young lad who had lived with his family in the area, who in recent months had tragically died in a police cell after being arrested for alleged theft. Some details had been spoken about as to how the young lad had managed to end his life in a police cell.

The television was on, then sport came on, which involved Manchester United playing. Only Paul-John followed football in the family, and he loved Liverpool. I switched the television off, and unusually Paul-John was unhappy about it. I reminded him it was Manchester United and he usually had something negative to say about the team.

Paul-John went and sat on the stairs, and when I went upstairs very shortly afterwards, I noticed he was in a bit of strop, which was unusual. I put it down to his age, and later realised he had gone to his room.

A short while later, I heard a thump type of noise, followed by a few lesser noises. I called up and asked Paul-John what he was doing. There was no reply, and unusually for me, I didn't follow it up. I was in the process of getting our 13-month-old grandson Phillip ready for bed.

Approximately 15 minutes later, Gareth asked Rachel to go upstairs and tell Paul-John to get ready to take them both to buy my birthday cards. (Our older children were working and had bought their own.) Rachel went upstairs to tell Paul-John, and shockingly found him hanging from the inside of his bedroom door.

We all heard a terrifying scream. I asked Gareth if he could go and see what the problem was. I thought it to be some insect as was usually the reason if Rachel screamed. However, Rachel called down, 'It's Paul-John...he is hanging!!!' Gareth and my older boys ran upstairs to where Paul-John was. I held on to my grandson Phillip as I was in denial of what I had heard. Gareth began working on Paul-John. He was not breathing.

That evening, Gareth and I were meant to go on a first aid course for the very first time. We were tired and decided not to go. Ironically, Gareth was doing first aid on Paul-John, the best way he knew how to.

Gareth ran onto the landing and shouted down to me, 'Dawn, he's not breathing, what can I do?' I had worked in a hospital for nine years, and had enough knowledge to tell him what to do. He continued to do mouth-to-mouth and chest compressions, whilst Andrew and Daniel went into the street and stopped cars, asking if anyone was trained in first aid.

They continued across the road to the local shop and also asked in there. Fortunately, a man from the area named Clive was trained in first aid, and came across to our home and continued where Gareth had left off.

By this time, I had asked Gareth to bring him downstairs, and lay him by the front door, still in denial, thinking that some fresh air would help. As Gareth carried Paul-John's lifeless body downstairs, I saw his face was blue, and he was floppy.

I had rung 999 the moment Rachel had alerted us to what had happened. They took seven minutes in all to arrive which seemed a lifetime.

The police arrived first and took over the chest compressions. The paramedics arrived, and continued, and then endeavoured to shock his heart. There were numerous attempts, and I heard one say, 'There is a faint heart beat.' They put him on life support and he was taken by ambulance to Morriston A&E Department. We were not allowed with him in the ambulance, as they needed the room to be able to continue working on him.

The police would not allow Gareth to drive to the hospital, as he was obviously in shock, so we were taken in a police car and followed the ambulance. I remember us crying, yet sure Paul-John would survive. We talked about how this time tomorrow Paul-John would be sitting up in bed, back to his usual self.

On arrival at the hospital, we were taken to the relatives' room. We had been in there just 18 months previously, when our middle son had met with an accident, and had had his spleen and a kidney removed. Gareth and I had spoken on how we had been in this room before, and Daniel had survived, so felt confident so would Paul-John.

The room was tiny, and had chairs, a table and a telephone. We were asked to ring family and friends and ask them to accompany us for support. Our older children were also with us in the room. I can remember pacing the corridor outside the room, waiting and hoping for some good news. A large machine was pushed into the resuscitation unit. On asking, I was told that it was an X-ray machine.

Eventually, after what seemed hours, but it wasn't, Gareth and I were called into the resuscitation unit. Doctors told us that Paul-John was critically ill, and may not pull through.

I looked at him laying there, with so many wires and tubes everywhere. He looked so vulnerable, yet there was no way in our minds that there could be a possibility that Paul-John may die.

We were asked a few questions about the events which took place earlier that evening, and we were told that Paul-John would be moved to ITU very soon, but to wait until someone called us to go there too.

Family and friends began to arrive at the hospital to support us. We were all numb as we tried to process how this could have possibly happened to such a sweet loving boy, our precious son, Paul-John.

That evening, Paul-John began to fit, which was so difficult to witness. At times I wouldn't be able to sit and watch him, and I would run out of the visitors' room. The doctors tried medication to stop the fits, but it didn't work.

Doctors approached Gareth and me to say the fits were the sign of severe brain damage. They continued to tell us how so very ill Paul-John was. We didn't get sleep that night; we just sat with Paul-John, hoping for change.

Close friends of ours, Dave Thomas and John Spiller, who were part of our church family, stayed with us, and took it in turns each night while we were at the hospital. We were and are so grateful for their love and support throughout the harrowing times.

By Thursday evening there was no improvement in Paul-John's condition. The doctors in Morriston had contacted a doctor in the Heath Hospital in Cardiff for help and advice as to how to stop the fitting. The advice given earlier in the day had not worked. We were told that Dr White would be coming to see Paul-John herself that evening, and assess him regarding the fitting. We were called to see doctors on ITU throughout the day for updates on Paul-John's condition.

There was a question I felt I needed to ask, but didn't have the courage to ask. My question was, 'Had anyone ever recovered from the amount of brain damage that Paul-John has?' It was later that evening that I nervously asked the question. The reply was stark and unwelcoming, as the doctor answered that he had not known of anyone to recover.

Later, while by Paul-John's bed in ITU, I saw the familiar metal trolley on wheels being wheeled in to an area where the curtains had been around the bed, just opposite where Paul-John lay. Having worked in the hospital for nine years previously, I was very familiar with the coffins on wheels. As I looked across the room, I tried to draw some comfort from the fact that the coffin trolley and our son, Paul-John, couldn't possibly go together.

Later that Thursday evening, Doctor White arrived to assess Paul-John, regarding the fits. We were so upset by the fits, as brown gunge poured from his nose, whilst his poor body shook. Doctor White advised us that she could prescribe medication to prevent the outward effects, but sadly, the fits would still continue in his brain, as the brain damage was causing them.

Other ITU doctors also asked to see Gareth and me to say that Paul-John's heart could give out at any time, and that he would be moved to a room of his own. This happened quite quickly, and they allowed me to lay on the bed with him and cuddle him the best I could, amongst all the lines and tubes attached to his precious body.

It was really difficult for us to update our older children, as we received the updates from the doctors. Gareth and I felt helpless to help them. We were all so distraught. We wanted to be able to give them encouraging updates, but there were none to pass on to them. Friday morning, however, we were able to give them a positive update. Paul-John had turned a small corner, and was breathing nineteen breaths a minute.

The doctors once again called us to speak with them, and they said Paul-John may live, but he would never wake up. They were considering administering a feeding tube, but he would be in a continuous vegetative state. The doctors said if Paul-John lived, we would eventually be able to take him home and care for him. This raised our expectations, and Gareth and I discussed how Gareth would finish work, and we would sell the house, and we would take care of him. As long as Paul-John would live, that's all that mattered.

We were so grateful for the prayers of all our friends, and we knew that nothing is too difficult for the Lord.

Gareth and I dozed in the chair that night by the side of Paul-John's bed. We had had very little sleep, and although we were sometimes awake, we had some rest throughout the early hours of Saturday morning.

It was about 8.30am when we heard the sister call us. We opened our eyes, and she said, 'I'm afraid, this is the day you say goodbye to Paul-John.'

We were so shocked, it was hard to take in, as there had been improvements the day before. I didn't want to believe her words, and questioned her, as Paul-John didn't look any different. The day before his colour had returned and he looked very much better. The truth was that Paul-John's brain stem had died in the night. It was only the machine that was keeping his organs going.

Her words were hard, and she said, 'I will give you five minutes, and then you'll need to wake your children up and tell them what's happened.' Daniel was sleeping on the floor in the corner, and Andrew, Rachel and Sarah had slept in the visitors' room.

It was the hardest thing to break this news to our children. They, like us, felt angry and found it hard to grasp this truth. We hugged and cried together, as only parents and siblings could, in our loss.

We were told to expect our GP to come and speak to us regarding organ donation. This is something Gareth and I had discussed on Thursday, after we were told Paul-John's heart may give out. However, we decided that all our children would have to be agreeable. We certainly didn't want to cause any more distress to them, and felt it important that we considered them in the decision-making.

We were also advised that tests would need to take place on Paul-John in order to confirm that his brain stem had died. Two doctors would carry out the tests independently of each other. This happened from about midday onwards. Very sadly, the findings were the same, and Paul-John's body was declared dead at 12 noon, Saturday, 7th March.

We signed the forms to agree to Paul-John's organs to be removed for transplant. We were then asked to leave the hospital as Paul-John would not be taken to theatre until the evening, as suitable recipients would need to be found.

We were to receive a phone call to ask us to return to the hospital later that evening to speak with the transplant co-ordinator, and to see Paul-John once again before going to theatre.

The ITU staff allowed many visitors over the days Paul-John was there. Many of our friends and family came to support us, for which we were very grateful. We wanted our home be an extension of that time, as Paul-John loved to welcome visitors, and would often make tea or coffee for them.

As we arrived home, the house began to fill up with family and friends. Gareth said to me, I want to speak with you and the children alone for a few minutes. We gathered in our front room, as Gareth gave us words of wisdom. He said, 'We now understand that we will grieve, but we each are going to grieve differently, and we need to allow each other to do that. We won't always agree with the way each of us grieve, but that is OK, but we need to allow it.' I remember feeling the relief amongst us in the room, as his words sunk in.

As word got around, many many people came to our home during the days leading up to Paul-John's funeral. Flowers, cards and letters poured in, which we were so grateful for. We would weep as we read the cards and letters each morning. The love, sympathy and empathy, words of wisdom, which are gifts money cannot buy, are often the best gifts of all.

Hundreds turned out for Paul-John's funeral. It was held at what we know now as City Church (Elim). Paul-John's classmates were asked to attend, at the discretion of parents. They each had a seat at the end of each row in the centre aisle, and as Paul-John's coffin was wheeled in, his classmates turned to face the aisle. I often wondered what their feelings were. It must be a time they will never forget. They were at that vulnerable age. I'm sure they had many questions in their minds.

The funeral was planned with what we felt Paul-John would like it to have been. It seemed surreal, as we looked at the coffin. How could it be possible that Paul-John's body was inside there?

It was not an easy task for Mick Walford and Mike Sutton-Smith to take the service, especially as Mick had spent many hours at our home playing on the floor with Paul-John as a younger child. Many said later, what a fitting service it was for Paul-John.

The days, weeks and months following were excruciatingly painful, as we as a family unit tried to navigate through this new normal, without Paul-John. Reality came mainly little by little as the daily reminders of Paul-John not being here sunk in.

It took me months to only put six plates out at meal times, rather than seven. When hanging clothes on the line, it was painful not to be hanging Paul-John's clothes out. All the daily tasks for him were no longer needed...each was a stark reminder that he had gone from our lives while on this earth.

Gareth, who was a tool setter for a sheet metal engineering firm, went back to work after two weeks. We shared our grief together, as we did with our older two children. We often reminded them that we were here to listen at any time.

Gareth and I had begun to rely on each other like never before. Although his employers gave him as much time as he needed with pay before returning to work, I knew that the longer Gareth was home with me, the more difficult it would be for him to return.

I remember that first morning he left for work. He told me I could change my mind. I just said, 'Go, you have to go!' I remember crying, knowing how difficult this was for us both.

Gareth found it very hard to be at work, but he has always been strong in his pursuit of what needs to be done. As he would be working in his workplace those first three months, as Paul-John was never from his thoughts, he began to write a line down, and later another one.

Gareth had not been interested in poetry before, but his lines were forming amazing poetry about Paul-John's life and the loss of him.

The gift lasted just three months and the poems are a gift in themselves. This is just one of many:

I will never have the pleasure of standing with you in the aisle
I will never meet your wife
and I'll never hold your child.
I'll never see that smile on your face again
All I feel inside is emptiness and pain.

I'll always have a feeling of loss inside my heart
Never fully understanding why we are apart
I will always have a peace inside
Because I know where you have gone
I will always own the privilege of calling you my son.

These poems have been used to help other bereaved parents identify their feelings of loss, as Gareth and I have sat and sought to help many over the years.

The hospital chaplain at the time was Nigel Griffin, who would often call us to speak to a newly-bereaved couple on the loss of their child. It seemed that whenever we reached out to help others in this way, a little more healing would take place in our lives.

As kind and thoughtful as people were, we all understand that people have to get on with their lives. We are also aware that after a person's funeral has taken place, the number of people calling to the home becomes less. For me this was particularly difficult, as I was home all day. However, close friends called which I was so grateful for. A friend living nearby, Christine Lucas, took me out at times in her car. I will never forget the kindness of such people. My friend June would pick me up and take me to her home for lunch on her day off.

I would often reach for the telephone whenever I felt I needed someone to talk to during the day. I remember one such time, I reached for the telephone and I heard an inner voice who I recognised as the Holy Spirit. 'Come away and talk with me,' I heard very clearly. I would sit with pen and paper and write down my thoughts and feelings. At those moments when I would become overwhelmed by grief, I would lay on my belly on the floor. At times I could not speak to the Lord, only groan, but He heard my every groan. There was never a time when I would get up from the floor without the Lord comforting me with a verse which He would bring to memory, or a song or hymn.

These times became a habit, and before I realised, hours would have gone by. I look back at this season as totally precious. I poured out my grief to the source of all comfort and strength, Who was my strength and stay.

One of the things which really bothered me was what was happening to Paul-John's body underground. I had carried my precious son in my womb for nine months, and after he was born, I cared for his every need. It was something I couldn't talk to family and friends about, as I didn't want to burden them further. I had the opportunity to talk this through so many times with my grief counsellor, someone who didn't know Paul-John. We were encouraged to have help in this way, which really did help in that first year.

One morning, as I was spending time with the Lord, I remember pouring out to Him my hurt regarding what was happening to Paul-John's body. I was crying at the time, my heart was so heavy, when again I heard that still small voice, 'But I am good with dust.' I recall being taken back and feeling so grateful, as the reality of those words sunk in. Never again was I to grieve over Paul-John's body, as I knew that some day mortal will take on immortality.

In the Autumn of 1997, a few months before Paul-John passed away, one of my best friends, June Phillips (who at the time was working in our community as a midwife) called to spend her lunchtime with me, as was usual. June asked me to pray for a little family in the community. Mum was heavily pregnant, and her second son aged three had terminal cancer.

I prayed for the family regularly. I didn't know who they were (as confidentiality needed to be upheld). Mum gave birth in December, and very sadly, her little three-year-old passed away the following month (January). I prayed for them in their awful loss, not knowing that as a mum, I too would pass this way just two months later.

The following June, my friend June asked if I would like to meet the lady who I had prayed for. Without hesitation I agreed, as I felt the need to speak with someone who was going through the same kind of loss as myself. June arranged a suitable time, and one morning she came and picked me up in her car to meet the lady at her home.

We knocked the door, and it was opened by Trish (name changed to keep identification private). We had never met, but we hugged each other tightly, and instantly felt a bond with each other. It was one of many meetings and phone calls, as we shared our thoughts and feelings, and we became good friends.

The following year, our second grandson was born, and I shared the news with Trish over the phone. Trish asked if we could bring our new grandson for her to see. At the end of the evening, I teased Trish about her being 'broody', as she had loved holding our grandson.

About six weeks later, Trish rung me and said, 'Guess what?' I replied, 'You're pregnant!' 'How did you know?' Trish asked. Out of my mouth came a verse from Isaiah 61v7 in the Bible, which speaks about a two-fold recompense reward. 'What are you saying, Dawn?' Trish asked. I replied, 'I'm not saying anything, but God is.'

Trish went for her first scan some weeks later, and it was revealed she was carrying twins. On her 20-week scan, it was also revealed Trish was carrying twin boys. How so faithful is God in bringing about His purposes.

The same month of June, when I first met Trish, I was given the opportunity to help out as a volunteer a few times a week in the CLC Bookshop which was a Christian bookshop in St Helen's Road. I was grateful for this opportunity, as it helped me in so many ways.

Three years later, the engineering company where Gareth had worked for 18 years suddenly folded.

Instead of feeling worried, we were excited, knowing that our great God was in control.

Gareth rung our house group leader Dave Thomas (who had stayed with us at the hospital when Paul-John was in ITU) to ask him and his wife to pray. Dave recalled how someone in our church had just opened a second Dry House in Swansea, and they were looking for staff.

Gareth had been involved with ACTS Soup Run in the city for quite some time, and had gone out very often with the manager of the Dry House. He contacted the manager and was asked to go for an interview on Sunday afternoon.

When Gareth arrived for the interview, he saw his name on the white board for shifts that week.

A few weeks later, I was asked to become a volunteer there. I enjoyed teaching the lads life skills, and getting to know them. I was later asked if I would be interested in being employed, but was told I would need to agree to do a diploma in welfare studies. Gareth and I went to college one day a week, and we passed and were awarded certificates.

As we were out in the car a few years later, I said to Gareth, 'I don't always feel I will be at the Dry House.' Gareth replied, 'I feel that too!' It wasn't that we were unhappy in our employment, but we both had a sense that we would move on fairly soon. The question was 'when, where, and how?' We didn't feel even to look, but knew that God would bring it about in His time.

A few short months later, we were at a wedding and sat on the same table as a staff member who we knew and who worked in Teen Challenge. He asked us how our jobs were going, and we shared with him of how we felt about moving on. ‘That’s interesting.’ he said, ‘Teen Challenge are looking for a couple.’ Teen Challenge liked to take on couples, even though men worked in the men’s centre and ladies worked in the ladies’ centre. We felt this was significant, and so we applied for the jobs.

The Lord’s plan for us was fulfilled, and we were there for six years, when the men’s centre moved to Leicester. I did not drive, so it was too difficult for me to stay. At the same time our eldest grandson moved back in with us and he needed to be looked after.

As we sat and looked for work online one day, a box popped up in my screen. It said the name of a private fostering company, and ‘Can YOU give a child a loving home.’ I looked across our front room where Gareth was sitting and read out what it said, with tongue in cheek. Gareth asked, ‘What does it say to do,’ and I replied, ‘Click on it.’ He said, ‘Click on it!’ We agreed to fill in our details and we expected to receive a phone call, which we did within days.

It was arranged that an assessor would call to see us in the weeks that followed, who went through lots of information with us. It so happened that our assessor was a Christian. Our God puts people in the right places to bring about His purposes. I will leave it there!

We went through panel some months later, and passed. We were told we would have a placement within two weeks, but this didn’t happen. Four months later, we were still waiting. We felt it was time to push forward, and it was explained to us that our local council was taking most of their fostering placements in house, to cut down on expenses. We felt it was right to apply to foster with them. We had to go through some of the assessment again, and we passed panel with them three months later.

Just after a week, the phone rang to say we had a placement. I was told they were twins, a boy and a girl aged six. I was given some details about them, and asked if we would like to go ahead, and of course I agreed. It was a weekend trial to see how it went, and a meeting was convened for Monday morning, as to the twins' future. Whether they would stay with us on a short-term placement or whether they would go to other foster carers with more experience.

There was no time to discuss anything with Gareth as he was working in Laugharne at the time about 40 miles away. It was so exciting to share this news with him by telephone. I had to go to a school and meet them half-an-hour before the end of the school day, and bring them home. I was absolutely elated, albeit a little apprehensive.

I arrived at the school, and was taken to a room and asked to wait for the headteacher to see me. A few minutes later, a social worker arrived and set about telling me how the twins didn't yet know they were coming home with me. They had been in a foster placement for a year, which had broken down.

A short while before the end of the school day, the twins were brought to the room where we were. They were introduced to me and were told they would not be returning to their foster home, but they would be staying the weekend with me and my husband.

I remember walking out of the school with Joe and Lizzy and the social worker, who was giving us a lift home. I held Joe's little hand, whilst Lizzy held the social worker's hand. We arrived home and I immediately showed them around the house, including their bedroom which they were to share for a little while at least, so that they had each other's company during the night.

I wanted to give Joe and Lizzy a fun-filled weekend in order that they didn't have much time to worry about their future. It was very uncertain, and continued to be for well over a year.

After an hour or so introducing them to our dog and generally helping them to settle in, I decided to take them to a local park.

I pushed them on the swings and joined in making sure they were safe on the climbing frames, etc. After a while it began to rain, so we left the park and waited in a nearby bus stop as the rain had become heavy. I knew that Gareth would be on his way home from work, so I rung him to see how much longer he would be. Gratefully, we didn't have to wait too long.

Joe and Lizzy were full of questions about Gareth. As they had had some bad experiences, I sought to put their minds at rest, and told them how funny, kind, and lovely Gareth was.

They were excited to meet him, and before long we saw the car in the distance coming toward us. We crossed the road, and there they were introduced to Gareth. Joe and Lizzy took to him straight away, for Gareth had them laughing straight away.

We had a lovely weekend with Joe and Lizzy, so much so that on Sunday evening they asked if they could stay with us, until they had their forever family.

They were sad on Monday morning as we dropped them at school. I kissed them goodbye and kept my mind occupied with the meeting I had to attend regarding their immediate future.

At the meeting I was asked to convey how the weekend had gone, whether there were any problems. I was able to say that it had gone really well, and how the children had warmed to us immediately.

The decision was made that Joe and Lizzy would stay with us on a short-term fostering placement. The arrangement was made that after school that day, the social worker would pick Joe and Lizzy up from school and take them to McDonald's for tea, when she would tell them that they would be returning to us.

I can remember feeling really excited about having them come to stay, and kept looking out of the window for them to arrive. I was asked by the social worker to make out it was a total surprise for me. Gareth was in work until later.

I can remember seeing the car arrive and standing on the door as they ran up the steps to our home, with excited squeals and big smiles, shouting, 'We are going to stay with you and Gareth until we have a forever family.'

The first three months were often challenging, as they had been through a lot in their early years. Settling in to someone else's routine and ways are never easy. They were traumatised as they did not know who, where or when they would go to next. We had the support of our family and social workers, and when we needed we would have help from a child psychologist who really guided us to unravel some behaviours.

Bedtime was particularly difficult, as they were unhappy for us to leave the bedroom. After some months, things began to improve slowly as we just loved them, yet choosing what behaviours to deal with one at a time. Joe and Lizzy slowly learned to trust us and over time faced many of their fears.

The following year we were approached by Social Services regarding Joe and Lizzy's future. The adoption link had fallen through, and Joe and Lizzy were at the end of the age range to be put back on the data base for adoption. We were asked if we would like to have Joe and Lizzy long term. Of course, we were delighted and accepted the offer.

At the meeting, we were advised of three options open to us. The first one was to continue to foster them as we were doing. The second option was to have Special Guardianship of Joe and Lizzy, or thirdly to adopt them.

For Gareth and me, there was only one option, and that was to take them out of care and give them a forever home with us. Everyone at the meeting agreed and were all hoping for this outcome. We had been told many times by social workers how we were such a great match, and how Joe and Lizzy looked like our family.

For the third time in two years, we were to be assessed again, although the adoption assessment was far more in depth than the fostering assessments we had been through. We also went to panel for the third time, and on February 4th, 2014, Joe and Lizzy became our very own children. We all enjoyed a morning in court to meet the judge, and for that official seal of approval to be made.

We have always told Joe and Lizzy how special adoption is, and how as God's people, we are all adopted into His family.

Over the years, Joe and Lizzy have brought us so much joy, and we continue to be so proud of them. They are doing so well in every aspect of their lives, but most particularly their faith in Jesus, who they have both trusted as their Saviour.

About three years ago, my friend June Phillips had called to see me shortly after Joe and Lizzy's birthday in January. In conversation, June asked me if I had seen Trish's recent post on Facebook regarding her twins' birthday and a photo of them. I said I had, and commented what handsome boys they were, now in their late teens. June continued...but Dawn, did you notice what date they were born on. I replied, 'Not really!' As I was thinking about what June was asking me, she replied, 'It's the same date as Joe and Lizzie's birthday!!!'

For a moment I just thought, 'I hadn't realised both sets of twins shared the same birthday,' until June reminded me about the verse I had shared with Trish regarding a two-fold recompense reward, when she shared with me about her pregnancy all those years before. The penny dropped! Not only was that verse for Trish all those years before, but the word was for Gareth and me too!

How alive and active is God's Word to us. We were blown away by this realisation, that God in His orchestrating of our lives, had put Trish's family and ours together to share and live out a verse of scripture, amidst totally heartbreaking situations, to bring about His purposes.

Isaiah 61 v 3

To all who mourn in Israel, he will give a crown of beauty for ashes, a joyous blessing instead of mourning, festive praise instead of despair. In their righteousness, they will be like great oaks that the LORD has planted for his own glory.

Revelation 21 v 1–7

Then I saw 'a new Heaven and a new Earth', for the first Heaven and the first Earth had passed away, and there was no longer any sea. I saw the Holy City, the new Jerusalem, coming down out of Heaven from God, prepared as a bride beautifully dressed for her husband. And I heard a loud voice from the throne saying, 'Look! God's dwelling place is now among the people, and he will dwell with them. They will be his people, and God himself will be with them and be their God. He will wipe every tear from their eyes. There will be no more death or mourning or crying or pain, for the old order of things has passed away.' He who was seated on the throne said, 'I am making everything new!' Then he said, 'Write this down, for these words are trustworthy and true.' He said to me: 'It is done. I am the Alpha and the Omega, the Beginning and the End. To the thirsty I will give water without cost from the spring of the water of life. Those who are victorious will inherit all this, and I will be their God and they will be my children.'

11

CHRIS'S STORY – GOD IN MY CANCER JOURNEY

I'm writing my story whilst we're all still in the midst of a global pandemic. Every day the news is dark and depressing. There has been much talk of the vaccine being the light at the end of the tunnel, but I've been reminded by a friend that, as Christians, we have a light IN the tunnel. In John 12v46 we read that Jesus says: *I have come as a light to shine in this dark world, so that all who trust in me will no longer wander in darkness.* (TPT)

Although most of us would prefer a life filled only with joy and blessings, we sometimes have to face difficult circumstances and tragedies. It's often during these times that God builds strength and character in us. Unexpected challenges, such as a cancer diagnosis or facing a global pandemic, can reveal what is most important in our lives, and they can lead us to the arms of the One who is the source of light and life.

Growing up

I was born and grew up in Swansea where my parents and I shared a house with my grandmother. She was a lovely Christian lady who took me to chapel every Sunday. It was in Sunday school where I was grounded in the Christian faith. I loved singing the hymns and songs and even did scripture exams every year! By the age of 14, I came to faith and was baptised. But it was at the age of 17 that I faced the first dark period in my life: my grandmother died. It was a huge loss, as she had always been there for me, and had been such a positive Christian influence over me. I missed her enormously, but I have cherished her example and commitment to the Lord to this day. My parents moved house a couple of years later, and by then I had started an undergraduate degree in Swansea University, studying biological sciences. When I graduated, I left home and started working as a scientific officer in the haematology department of the Heath Hospital in Cardiff.

Meeting my soulmate

My husband, Mike, and I first met at the age of 16 when his family moved to Swansea from Hereford. He attended a different church from me, but our youth groups interacted at different events. But it was when I moved to Cardiff that we became good friends. He had graduated from Cardiff University and was working in the city centre. Our friendship developed, and we were married in 1977 when we were both in our twenties. Our first house was in Rhiwbina, and we started to go to the local Baptist church. A few years later, our daughter Sophie was born, and then in 1983 our son, Alex, came along.

Being members of a vibrant church was such a blessing at this time when our children were young. There were always people on hand to offer practical or spiritual advice when needed. Our daughter Sophie was very lively, to put it mildly, and I remind her of this when she finds her own daughter a challenge! But it was when she was only eleven months old that I faced my second big challenge. In early December 1981, my father died after a very short illness. As you can imagine, it was a difficult Christmas for my mother and us, but having our little girl crawling around and making us smile was a God-send.

Moving on

It was when our children were in primary school that we started to think about moving back to Swansea. My mother was finding it hard living alone, and so far away from us. Mike's parents were now very involved in Parklands Church, in Sketty Park, and his dad had recently become the pastor of the church. Having prayed, it seemed to make sense to try and move closer to our family in Swansea. This was confirmed when I was given a verse by a friend, who didn't know where I was born. It was from Zephaniah 3v20: *At that time, I will gather you; at that time, I will bring you home.*

It was exciting and thrilling to have a specific promise that God was going to bring us home. It didn't happen immediately, but after a couple of years, and two interviews, Mike was successful in getting a job as a lecturer in West Glamorgan Institute of Higher Education, and we moved to Swansea in 1988. We attempted to buy a house in an area close to the sea, but the purchase fell through at the last moment. This was really disappointing at the time, but we finally moved to Sketty, and started attending Parklands Church. We were one of a number of couples who arrived at a time when the fellowship was praying for an influx of younger couples. We quickly found our niche in the fellowship, hosting a house-group in our home, Mike became a deacon and later was elected on to the eldership team. I was involved in starting a mother/toddler group, was active in the worship team, and now a member of the pastoral team.

It has been a privilege to see the fellowship grow, both in number and maturity, and to see God at work in many individuals' lives and situations. Our children were very happy growing up in the beautiful city of Swansea, and both moved on through secondary school and later to university. They are now both married, and have families of their own. We have been blessed with three beautiful grandchildren whom we love dearly.

A difficult year

My cancer story begins at the end of October 2016 when we were visiting my daughter and family who live in Germany. It had been a somewhat difficult year as both of our mothers were elderly, frail and in poor health. Being my mother's carer, I was feeling the strain, as I had increasingly spent more time looking after her.

Towards the end of August, at the age of 95, she passed away following her third heart attack. She was very close to both our children, and we were so grateful that she had seen our daughter that weekend, as Sophie and her family had been visiting us. Our son had also come to Swansea when he knew she had been taken ill, and had visited her in hospital just before she died. Mike and I were privileged to be with her when she passed away peacefully.

After the funeral, a few weeks later in September, we had the joy of welcoming our new grandson into the world. He was born on my birthday, to our son and daughter-in-law in Surrey. I was sad that mum hadn't lived to see William, but glad that our son had whispered his name to her the last time Alex saw her. My dad was named William, so she would have been thrilled to bits.

We had planned a holiday later in September, our first break as a couple for quite a while. We were also looking forward to spending time visiting our family in Germany the following month. Our daughter had met her husband in France where they were both working as French assistants in university. They married a few years later, and eventually settled in a lovely area of Germany near the Luxembourg border, where they now work as secondary school teachers.

The Best-Laid Plans...

We had been enjoying our time in Germany with our two grandchildren who were five and two at the time, when one afternoon, I had terrific pain in my abdomen. It lasted for about 90 minutes but then subsided. I had never had a pain like this before, but as it had gone, I didn't want to make a fuss. However, my daughter insisted that we visit her GP later in the afternoon. Having described my symptoms, he seemed to think I had gall bladder problems, and recommended that we visit A and E at the local hospital. After being examined there, the doctor concluded I had acute pancreatitis and should be admitted. This wasn't in our plan at all, and I began to feel very vulnerable. I couldn't speak German, and although the staff spoke a little English, I felt very alone.

The following day, I had a scan, and the radiologist reported that my gall bladder looked reasonably ok. I breathed a sigh of relief, but there was more! He said, 'There's a shadow in your pancreas which needs further investigation.'

My heart sank at this point and I began to panic. Immediately I thought of my father who died when I was in my mid-twenties. He was roughly the same age as me when he was diagnosed with cancer, and it had spread through his body. His health declined very rapidly, and within five or six weeks of his diagnosis he died. It was Friday, and I had to wait until Monday for a more detailed CT scan, which hopefully would clarify the situation.

As you can imagine, it was a very difficult weekend. I was in a room with two other ladies who couldn't speak English, so I felt very isolated. I didn't understand what was happening to me. I spent most of Saturday in tears, wondering what the future would hold. Would I live to see my grandchildren grow up? The youngest was only six weeks old, and I barely knew him.

One of the lessons I learned during the difficult times in hospital and during my treatment was how

God was able to encourage and comfort me through scripture verses given at just the right time. He has never ceased to amaze me with the love and care He has shown in such a timely way.

The morning after receiving such devastating news, the words I read in my daily devotional were such a comfort. God spoke to me through Joshua 1v9: *Be strong and very courageous for the Lord your God is with you wherever you go.* I didn't feel strong at that moment, I can assure you, but I clung on to the promise that God was with me!

I hardly slept on that Saturday night, so felt very tired and low the next day, but again, in my devotional, God spoke to me through Psalm 18v2: *The Lord is my rock, my fortress and my deliverer; my God is my rock, in whom I take refuge.* I felt encouraged that God reiterated that He was there with me, despite the circumstances, which were overwhelming!

So, Monday arrived, and I was sent for a CT scan in the morning. We had to wait until our son-in-law was home from work to receive the results, as neither of us could speak German. Later that afternoon the doctor requested to see us. Unfortunately, the news was not what we wanted to hear…there was a large tumour in my pancreas which needed to be removed. They had even booked me in for an operation on the following Friday!!!

Crying Out to God

I felt numb, as if this was happening to someone else.

And then the tears came. Mike, my son-in-law, Matthias, and I clung together and cried. How was I going to be able to go back to my daughter and tell her this news, and tell our son in Surrey that I had been diagnosed with cancer?

Again, the Lord spoke into the situation. That evening I read 1 Peter 5v7: *Cast all your anxiety on him because He cares for you.* Reading these verses at this particular time was not a coincidence. I had been a worrier, and looked for comfort in verses like this in the past. God understood what I was going through and how I felt. He was assuring me of His presence, I could bring all my cares and worries to Him, and He would take care of me.

'Thank you Lord for your amazing love and faithfulness. Please help me to keep trusting You, despite my circumstances. Amen.'

I didn't think I would sleep well on that Monday night, but I slept for five hours, and on Tuesday morning, my reading was from Psalm 145v18, *The Lord is near to all who call upon Him, to all who call upon Him in truth.* 'Lord, you know what's going on in my life at the moment. As I call out to you, please give me wisdom to make a decision about the operation. Should I have it in Germany, or not?'

It was so tempting to have the op on Friday. I wanted this 'alien' inside of me removed as soon as possible. But it was really hard being in an environment where I couldn't ask questions or understand fully what was being said to me. We needed great wisdom!

Tuesday, 1st November was All Saints' Day and is a bank holiday in Germany. Thankfully, I was allowed to go to our daughter's house for the day. It was so lovely to be outside the hospital and in a familiar environment. We talked, cried and prayed together with our family, and asked God to lead us in our decision-making. The hospital needed to know whether to keep the operating theatre free for Friday. Lots of phone calls, emails and texts were made, and God was so gracious in leading us in all of this.

I phoned a doctor friend, Mary, to ask for advice, as she had suffered with cancer herself. I was surprised when she said she was speaking to me from Switzerland, where she was supporting her sister who was seriously ill. She said that coping with a serious illness in a foreign country was very difficult.

She knew we had family and friends in Swansea who would support us, and a wider church family who would pray and support us too. And, by the way, 'Did we know that Morriston Hospital in Swansea was a specialist centre for pancreas treatment?' Wow! We were so encouraged by that news!

The hospital in Germany was a general hospital, and although I had good care there, they weren't a specialist centre. It seemed that God was leading us to return home! She also told us that a mutual friend of ours, whom we knew from years ago, was now head of cancer services in Wales, and would we like her telephone number? Thank you, Lord, for answering prayer! All these signposts gave us the confidence that it was the right decision to return home.

When I returned to the hospital that evening, I rang my friend Barbara in Swansea to tell her the news of my diagnosis. Our prayer triplet of Barbara, Ali and I, usually met Tuesday evenings, and I knew they would pray for me.

When we arrived back at the ward, I was told that a single room had become available, and as I had not been sleeping well, would I like to move into it that evening? 'Thank you, Lord, you do more than we ask or imagine!'

Going Home

I slept very well that night. The following day, I was discharged from hospital, as I had decided to return to Swansea for my operation and was feeling well enough to leave. I was very happy to go back to the familiar surroundings of our daughter's house. There was a lot to organise. We had driven to Germany, but it was obvious that we had to return by plane. So, there were phone-calls to our insurance provider, flights to be booked and transport to organise for the return to Swansea from Heathrow. Also, our friend from cancer services had recommended a surgeon and paved the way for a consultation with him when we arrived home. So, our son organised for all my medical reports from the hospital to be translated into English, and we had to courier copies of my scans to the surgeon in preparation for my appointment.

All this was organised within two days, which was an amazing feat, but God had prepared the way for us. My reading that day from my devotional was from

Roman 8v37: *Yet among all these things, we are more than conquerors through Him who loved us.* And a comment from the writer: 'Whenever a trial comes against you, always remember: this too will pass! Be confident that during the trial you will learn something that will help you in the future.'

Within a week of my diagnosis, we were on our way home! It was an emotional time saying goodbye to our daughter and family. The gravity of the situation was hitting home, and the prospect of what lay ahead was unnerving. At the same time, we were already so aware of God's provision in all the practical arrangements that we knew He was walking through this valley with us. The night before we left, my reading was Matthew 19v26: *With man this is impossible, but with God all things are possible.*

The return trip was uneventful and straightforward, the highlight being able to see our youngest grandson, William, when we arrived back home in Swansea. He was now seven weeks old, what joy!! These precious times become more important when we realise how fragile life is!

The following week was a busy one with visits from family and friends, gifts of flowers, meals and cakes and uplifting prayer times with church family. During this time we received many encouraging verses of scripture when, again, God promised to undertake for us. We gained such strength from these times of fellowship and prayer, and the practical outworking of God's love and light through His people.

Psalm 27v1 reads:

The Lord is my light and my salvation, whom shall I fear?
The Lord is the stronghold of my life, of whom shall I be afraid?

And another comment at the time from my daily devotional:

'Life will disappoint you…things will happen that you don't expect, so you have to believe in the power of God. He will never allow more to come than we can bear. We don't understand why, but we know God has reasons and we can get through it.'

I'm so thankful for God's voice through scripture. His word came alive to me during this time, assuring me of His presence, power and authority over all that was going on in my life. I felt in my heart that, although I didn't choose to be in this situation, God was with me and would achieve something good from it.

Preparing for Surgery

During that week we had our first meeting with Prof Bilal, my surgeon. He instilled huge confidence in us both, at the same time being quite frank that the operation would be a long one. It involved removing two thirds of my pancreas, my spleen (as the tumour was touching it on one side) and my gall bladder, and there could be some risks from the procedure.

However, he concluded that 'he had never lost anyone on the operating table yet', for which we were very grateful!! He requested more blood tests and scans before he would see me a second time to discuss the results.

My next challenge was having an MRI scan. I had never had one before and was quite anxious about it as I suffered from claustrophobia! The thought of being enclosed in a metal tube for 30 minutes filled me with terror.

However, God sent me an angel in the form of a lady from church called Paula, who was lead nurse in the radiology department. She talked me through the procedure and even offered to show me the scanner beforehand to settle my nerves! I felt God had put her there for such a time as this. She also knew my surgeon and reinforced my opinion that he was an approachable man who was skilled at his job. Thank you, Lord!

I was told that I could take a CD with me for the scan. The machine is very noisy, so the music played over the earphones is a distraction. I've always found inspiration and consolation in Christian music, so it seemed natural for me to choose a CD by a Christian artist. It really helped me to get through the scan without too much angst. I still turn to worship songs when I need to find solace, as well as encouragement.

I've been interested to discover recently that many of the Psalms are in fact laments, which would have been sung in times of distress. In singing them, the psalmist finds consolation in God's word. This was certainly true for me, listening to God's word through song as I lay in the scanner! As Pete Greig said in his book, *God on Mute*, 'Honest lament can express a vibrant faith; one that has learned to embrace life's hardships as well as its joy, and to lift everything to the Father in prayer.'

When we went for the results of the scans, we were relieved to hear that the surgeon was confident that he could operate to remove the tumour. He hoped to do so by keyhole surgery which would mean a quicker recovery, but emphasised the complexity of the procedure. This might mean him having to operate conventionally. He offered a date for the end of November which meant being admitted in ten days. The reality of the situation began to hit me. It was a step into the unknown, facing major surgery, and not knowing what the outcome would be.

Again, God spoke to me through a prayer in my daily reading: 'Lord, you know me inside out. You see my strengths and weaknesses. I trust You to be working and equipping me to face the challenges of today and tomorrow. Help me to be brave, knowing that You are with me. Amen.' It couldn't have been more relevant!

The next ten days were a flurry of activity which was a good thing, as it distracted me from what was ahead. We were so grateful to return to church on Sunday and to feel the strength of prayer support from our church family. We met up with family and had coffee with friends. All the normal things that everybody does suddenly become very precious when life seems so fragile. We made plans for our daughter to fly over from Germany just before my op, and my son and family drove down from London too.

Anyone who has been admitted to hospital knows that there is a lot of waiting around! I was admitted on Friday afternoon, booked in, and my surgery was planned for the following morning. In the meantime, Prof Bilal visited and said that a bed had been booked in the High Dependency Unit (HDU) for after the op. If an emergency came in, and the HDU bed was needed, then my op might be postponed. This filled me with dread as I had psyched myself up for the op in the morning, so this became an urgent matter for prayer. My husband had set up a WhatsApp group with a number of family and friends who had promised to pray for us during and after the seven-hour op. We were so humbled and grateful for this! The following morning the HDU bed was still available, thank God, and I was taken mid-morning down to the operating theatre. As a person who could so easily worry, I felt an amazing peace and felt I was being upheld by the prayers of God's people.

Learning to Live with Cancer

When I opened my eyes in the recovery room after the op, my family were there to greet me. They laughed when I remarked, 'Oh, I've had a wonderful sleep!' The surgeon had told them that the operation wasn't without complications, but had gone well! And remarkably, there was no need to be taken to HDU, and so instead, I was taken to a general surgery ward.

I returned to the ward with a drip and tubes attached to various parts of my body. These included a nasal-gastric tube which made my throat really sore.

Thankfully, after pleading with my doctor, this was removed first. Also, there was a catheter, a wound drain and an intravenous drip for analgesia. I viewed the removal of each one of these tubes as a milestone in my recovery, and a step forward to my return home. However, I didn't expect or anticipate what happened next.

My heart decided to start beating irregularly. It felt very peculiar and frightening. The doctor was concerned, as he thought it might be an indicator of a blood clot. He advised a CT scan to check for this. So, I was rushed down to the scanner where, thankfully, my friend Paula was on duty! An immediate answer to my arrow prayer for help! She wheeled me into the room and I was scanned straight away. The scan was clear, and after being put on a 24-hour heart monitor and treated with medication, the problem disappeared. The cardiologist concluded that my arrhythmia was due to trauma from the extensive time in surgery. Thankfully, the rest of my time in the surgical ward wasn't quite so dramatic, and with each day, there were small steps of improvement towards a long-awaited discharge.

Five days later, I was discharged from hospital, even though I was told to expect to be there for at least a week! It was so lovely to be home and sleep in my own bed! A nurse came every day for a week or so to give anticoagulants and dress my wound. The latter was quite impressive, by the way, as the surgeon couldn't proceed using the keyhole technique after all, and had to open me up!

Lessons learned

My recovery wasn't without complications, but looking back I can see God's hand in it all, and He has taught me so much through my cancer diagnosis!

I have found a new normal in my life. I know cancer has changed me; I have the physical scars to prove it. I now have to take regular medication, and because the cancer had spread to my liver, I'm currently being treated with monthly injections to prevent further growth and spread.

But it has changed me in other ways too. It has made me grateful for things that perhaps I took for granted before. For each new day, for the joys of walking in God's beautiful creation, for seeing the world through the eyes of our grandchildren, and for spending precious time with our family and friends.

Cancer has also given me a desire to journey beside others walking a similar path. I have been a regular visitor and fundraiser at our local Maggie's centre. Here, I've found a calm, friendly and uplifting space where professionals offer support and advice. There have been positive conversations with other patients, and opportunities to share my story with them, over a cup of tea.

Cancer has forced me to draw deep upon God's grace and strength. His power in my own weak, imperfect and broken vessel. *But we have this treasure in jars of clay to show that this all-surpassing power is from God and not from us* (2 Corinthians 4v7). And I've realised that even though we might be walking through the deepest, darkest valley, facing pain and suffering, we have the comfort of knowing that God is present in the midst of it all.

Mike's Perspective

We have decided to add a carer's perspective, as cancer isn't something that only affects the patient. Mike was also profoundly affected by Chris's diagnosis, and takes up the story.

We had been married 40 years in June 2017 and, as you can see from what Chris has written, we had been through many experiences in life, spiritually as much as physically, and I would say that we were 'mature' Christians. But what happened in 2016 shook us to the core. Our world was blown apart by the suddenness and severity of the news we received.

I confess that while Chris was in hospital, I spent many hours alone in my room at our daughter's house, shouting at God and arguing with Him. I couldn't contemplate Chris going through the pain of treatment or the thought of losing her, especially at a time when I thought we could be spending more time together, with each other and with our family.

Those who know me as an elder in our fellowship at Parklands church in Swansea may be surprised to read how I responded. Some of the phrases they might have expected me to write would be, 'It's tough, but I must accept God's will,' or 'I'm facing our suffering joyfully.' But my humanity won through. And this was the first lesson I learned on our journey through cancer. Do you know what? God is bigger than my rantings at Him. My Christian upbringing had been influenced by the attitude that, as a Christian, one should never admit to having problems or being angry or upsct. But to be honest, I was feeling rubbish, and out of control.

God understands

I felt guilty at first about how I spoke to my Father. Then I remembered the Psalmist's words in which he expressed his deepest anguish. In Psalm 22 we read: *My God, my God, why have you forsaken me? Why are you so far from saving me, so far from my cries of anguish? My God, I cry out by day, but you do not answer, by night, but I find no rest.*

These are words Jesus uttered on the cross. Remembering these words, I felt that God was saying that He wanted me to be real with Him. After all, as Psalm 139:2 says, He knows our thoughts from afar off, so there's no point in trying to hide them from Him.

I can do this – or can I?

The second lesson I learned within hours of the news having been broken to us, was how much of a control freak I am. Every problem has a solution. Or in my case, every solution deserves a problem!! But what on earth could I do about what Chris was going through? That was the crux of the matter! On earth I could do very little. I felt powerless. It was only in Heaven that the solution could be found. Handing over Chris to the Lord was perhaps the hardest thing that I have ever had to do in my life. Standing by her, and with her, and holding her, was all I could do.

Yes, there was much for me to do, and I dived into the activity! Arranging flights home, discussing with our insurance company what help they could offer, getting Chris's medical reports translated from German into English, booking a low loader to return my car to Swansea, deciding where the best place for treatment would be, telling our friends and family about the devastating news – all this kept me occupied, but not distracted.

It's only in looking back, that we can see how great and gracious our God had been during that episode. As Chris said, He hasn't told us He would take us out of the difficult situations in our lives. But He has promised to be with us through it all. And He was. No Heavenly choirs, or visions of being lifted up above the mire we found ourselves in. But a gentle peace and Father's hand being evident in the people He had put on our path to help us, even down to the name of the doctor who cared for Chris after her operation. He was called Christian! And a lovely Christian nurse who was a channel of God's care and comfort to Chris as she recovered.

All healing is miraculous. Another key lesson, which I think I knew anyway, was that God can choose to heal in different ways. Yes, I prayed for a miracle of immediate and mind-blowing healing. And yet God had a different plan. He has given people talents in research, diagnosis, treatment and medication to help us in our times of sickness, and to channel His healing power.

Prayer – ancient and modern in harmony. Prayer became more real, relevant and critical. I wondered how I could get the message out to ask our friends to support us in prayer. My thinking was that God has given us technology, which can be a force for good, as much as having the potential for malevolent outcomes.

So, WhatsApp seemed the way forward. I set up a group with our closest Christian friends, whom we knew would invest their time, and themselves, in prayer for us both. These were friends and close family from around the country, and around the world, whom God had placed on our journey through life. With our friends in Australia, praying when we were sleeping, we realised that we had 24/7 prayer cover!

We are so grateful to Father for providing such lovely friends and family to support us, and with whom we could share our deepest fears and anguish.

In Luke 5:17-26 we read the story of the paralysed man whose friends wanted Jesus to heal him. But the crowd was so thick that they couldn't bring him to Jesus.

We read how they carried him up onto the roof, removed some roof tiles and let him down right in front of Jesus. And Jesus healed him! This became the model we have followed. On many occasions during the diagnosis and treatment, we felt totally helpless, unable to pray for ourselves, and were reliant on our friends bringing us to the feet of Jesus.

This approach has proven so powerful that we have encouraged others to 'rip the roof off' in order to bring those in need to Jesus in prayer. We called on our friends, not only to lower us gently to the feet of Jesus, but also to pray for those treating Chris. We told Professor Bilal before Chris's big op that he probably hadn't ever had so many people praying for him! After all, if he was to be the hands of God in cutting out the tumour and various internal organs, then he needed to have a steady hand and a clear mind to make the right decisions! Faithful God and faithful friends.

As Chris said earlier, not only did she survive the operation, but, despite a couple of hiccoughs, she didn't need intensive care support immediately afterwards. And she was able to come home earlier than the doctors had predicted.

After Chris had had her operations (she also had a liver resection in June 2017), I asked members of the WhatsApp group if they were happy for me to wind it up. They replied unanimously – Keep it going! And how wonderful it has proven to be. Others in the group have also experienced challenges such as a cancer diagnosis, personal illness and family problems. I am delighted to say that we have been able to swap places with them, by holding the ropes on the bed and letting them down through the roof to the feet of Jesus. What a privilege!!

Our journey continues. It's a real rollercoaster! Every scan and consultation raises questions and concerns about Chris's future health. Has God healed Chris? No, not entirely. Is he healing her? We believe He is – through the regular monitoring and the monthly hormone injections she is currently having to control the growth of the remaining tumours in her liver. Has our faith been shaken? Faith in my own ability to manage things has definitely been shaken! But our faith that God is working and has been with us every step of the way is assured.

Walking together

And what about the future? We believe God has taught us so much more about Himself, His character and His love through this cancer journey. Our desire is that, through sharing our experience, we can hopefully help others travelling a similar path.

Many will have seen the TV programmes of Michael Palin's trips around the world, and it is lovely to view his experiences from a distance on our screens. But how much better it would be to actually walk alongside him. We don't want to stand on the side-lines watching others struggle with their problems.

We want to walk alongside them, holding their hand, and sharing from our backpack of experiences. We know what they're going through! More importantly, we KNOW how God provides, and supports, and heals, and loves, and keeps on giving, until He brings us to our ultimate place of healing – His presence.

When Chris was diagnosed with cancer, it plunged both of us into a darkness that we had never experienced before, and one which we didn't think we could navigate. But Jesus is the light who shows us the way in every challenge we have to face. If you are facing a dark time in your life at the moment, our prayer would be that, in reading our story, you will find the hope that comes from knowing Jesus. He is the

Light of the world, and when we know Him, we will never walk in darkness, but will have the Light of life.

Mike and Chris Day

12
JOSHUA'S STORY

Holly

I have known God's plan for my life since I was a child – all I have ever wanted to be, and felt called by God to be, is a mother. What I have now come to realise is that my understanding of the term mother was not the same as God's. I could plan my life as much as I wanted, but I have come to understand that God had a different and better plan in mind.

In 2011 we had our first son Oscar. Two years later, according to our plan, it was time for baby number two. But we struggled to conceive; every month brought disappointment until it was all I could think about. One day I remember realising we had been struggling through this alone and not seeking God. I asked God to give us the baby we so desired. The very next month I had fallen pregnant!

All progressed as usual until it came to the 20-week scan. We arrived together with little Oscar, full of excitement to show him his little brother on the screen. The sonographer was very quiet. She couldn't get a good picture, she said. She asked us to go to the café and come back in thirty minutes. Thinking nothing of it, off we went. It was when we returned, the sonographer gently informed us that she had seen a few anomalies on the scan and the consultant would see us straight away. Time seemed to stop.

The next month was a whirlwind of appointments. We were initially informed our baby had spina bifida and we were consumed by thoughts of caring for a disabled child and all that would entail. I was sent for an amniocentesis in Cardiff and it was through this that we discovered the full diagnosis – a genetic condition called triploidy. What did that mean? It was 'incompatible with life' we were told, ‘most people choose to terminate the pregnancy at this point’. We were utterly devastated.

That said, God was with us and His perfect love casts out all fear. I wish I could say that we felt no fear at all, but we did have an overwhelming sense of God-given peace. I knew I didn't want to terminate the pregnancy and thankfully Mark felt the same. In hindsight, I can say without doubt this was entirely the right decision to make for ourselves, but honestly at the time it was hard, we considered all other options.

God sustained us through the next few months with support from our family and church family. There were so many people praying for us. We felt surrounded by love, and the peace was hard to understand.

Although it wasn’t expected that our baby would live for long, if at all, we still had to make plans for delivery and potential after-care. The regular scans and appointments continued.

One thing I hadn't been prepared for was the pain and difficulty of having an obvious pregnancy that everyone wanted to speak to you about – even strangers in the street. Each time I would have to make the decision whether to tell the truth or just go along with the joy of the other person. I would be asked all the usual questions like 'when are you due?', 'Are you all prepared?', 'Is Oscar excited to be a big brother?'

Then afterwards, the postman asking me how the baby is, and having to avoid the local shop so I didn't have to explain where the baby was. All seemingly harmless questions, but so difficult to answer.

In my thirtieth week of pregnancy I started to feel very tired – more than normal pregnancy tiredness. Sickness and swelling followed. By 35 weeks our baby – we had decided to name him Joshua – was growing well, but I was not well. One evening I couldn't get out of bed to greet some guests. I knew something wasn't right. The next morning, I went to be checked out at the hospital whilst Mark took Oscar to church. 'Probably just dehydration,' the midwife informed me as she took a blood sample. Twenty minutes later my bed was surrounded by doctors. It was serious. Possibly HELLP syndrome or acute fatty liver of pregnancy. The only cure was to deliver the baby as soon as possible. I was alone and scared. It didn't feel real. I needed to have an emergency Caesarean and probably would have to have a general anaesthetic. This was scary as it meant that if by some miracle Joshua was born alive, it might not be for very long – possibly just a few breaths and I might miss it. Somehow, I knew that he would be born alive and that we would get to meet him.

Mark was now with me, but I had to give myself over to the care of the medical team then...trust, trusting God that he would carry me through and His perfect will be done.

Mark

I wasn't allowed into the operating theatre, but because I made a fuss they let me sit in the anaesthetics room with windows into the operating theatre. I kissed Holly on the head and told her I was proud of her as she went down, both of us expecting it to be a straightforward C-section. Joshua was brought out to me soon after – very much alive!

He was wrapped up and weighed. I held him and cried, happy tears and sad tears. We were surrounded by doctors and midwives in the strangest of little rooms, but this was our time. He was perfect. Not perfectly formed...an extra toe, a large opening to his spine and an incomplete heart which was to make his life very short, but he was perfect. I had to check and ask if he was still breathing, so shallow were his breaths and little noise he made. Over and again I would whisper through my tears, 'Daddy loves you, Mummy loves you, God loves you.' I just kept on talking to him and singing to him whilst in my arms. What I sang I can't recall. I just knew my responsibility to let this little boy know he was so dearly loved, and to let him, in his own way, tell me the same.

I was though worried about Holly. Time went on for ever and they just kept on trying to reassure me. At one point I saw them put sheets of white paper up to cover the windows. They would only give me vague answers about what was going on. Holly had carried him for 35 weeks. This was our time: Joshua and me. Desperate as I was to share these moments with Holly and be a family together, I knew I needed this time alone with my boy. I was to hold him close. This was a time entrusted to me. I will always be thankful for that opportunity. In those two hours I learnt more than ever: of the value of life, of how we should hold each other close, of how God sees us so perfectly formed, of where our strength comes from.

Holly finally came out after surgical complications, and was soon able to open her eyes well enough to see Joshua faintly. I told her he is beautiful, but she needed to rest. I lay him next to Holly, nestled in her arm. We were so fortunate to have the four-bed high dependency unit all to ourselves. It was late but what could I do…Do I sleep? Can I sleep? Can I stay awake? But then peace, and I slept.

Joshua breathed his last, one moment around 2.00 am, six hours after he was born, whilst we were both asleep. I stirred and Holly had too. She did her best to call over to me, 'Is he still breathing.' It was hard to tell, but it was soon clear and the doctor confirmed it. I sat, and Holly lay, in sorrow, but in peace.

Holly was extremely tired so didn't remember a lot of this time, and as it turned out she was still bleeding inside. A blood test came back which showed worrying signs and she was rushed back into theatre. I was left alone, with Joshua in the cold cot. 'Should be 40 minutes or so,' they said. I can't describe the way I felt as time dragged on, except to say I hope I never know it again.

Four hours later Holly was brought back through, still mostly unaware, all wired up and drugged up, but it was the best sight. Later I asked the surgeon what happened. He said, 'She just kept bleeding and we couldn't get it to stop. We gave her eight litres of blood and two litres of platelets. It was touch and go.'

The next day I headed home for a couple of hours, and as I returned to Holly, a huge rainbow arched across between the hospital and the sea – a sure sign of the assurance we have in God's promises to never leave us or forsake us.

Holly

I was so sleepy after the caesarean; I could barely keep my eyes open. I couldn't sit up, but I do have a precious memory of holding Joshua. He was so quiet but he occasionally made a little noise; he didn't cry. I held him like that and finally couldn't hold off the sleep any longer. I woke to find him still, beside me, and I knew he was gone.

It was in the hospital bed afterwards I felt the presence of Jesus so strongly. It was so comforting to feel Him close by. He sustained me through the week I spent in hospital recovering. He 'fed' me when I could not eat or drink for several days.

We played the worship song 'Oceans' every night as we went to sleep and I felt it healing me, bringing me peace. When we couldn't pray, we would listen to worship music, which lifted our eyes up, onto Jesus and away from our situation.

***

It was in the hospital that I realised I would never be able to give birth to another baby, but that didn't stop us from having another child. We had always wanted to become foster carers one day, but now the thought of adoption came into our hearts.

A little while later we read the book *Home For Good* by Krish Kandiah and I felt the Holy Spirit speaking to me so clearly. This was God's plan for us. The day the adoption social worker came to visit us for the first time was (unbeknown to us) the day our daughter Sofie was born, five minutes down the road, in the hospital where I worked and had given birth to Joshua only six months previously.

The pain and loss experienced by her birth mother is not lost on us and I recognise the huge privilege of raising another person's child as our own. Sofie is our daughter in all respects and we love her unconditionally.

Many people congratulate us on doing a wonderful thing in adopting Sofie and comment on how lucky she is to have come into a new and loving family. We feel it is we who are the lucky ones. God who has entrusted us with her care. Both Sofie and Joshua are treasures that were 'hidden in the darkness' and we are so thankful to God for them.

Mark and Holly

When we didn't have strength, God used his faithful servants. They came in different shapes and sizes...the truly kind paediatrician who stayed long after her shift had finished to support us, June turning up unexpectedly to wait with me whilst Holly was in surgery that second time, Mark's dad being on the end of the phone while he wept, Sue and Bri coming to bless Joshua as he lay in the cold cot, Holly's parents for doing whatever was required, hugging Oscar when I'd go home from the hospital, friends and family that couldn't understand but chose to stand with us, friends and family who shared their own stories, the various people who travelled or took time out to attend the funeral despite the pain of seeing us carry a wicker coffin so small, Matt (overseeing his first funeral) speaking of God's love through it all, and the various messages of support.

God is love and is part of us all. His love seeps out of us when we do not hold it in. Thank you to all those who allowed that love to seep out.

In all this you greatly rejoice, though now for a little while you may have had to suffer grief in all kinds of trials. These have come so that the proven genuineness of your faith – of greater worth than gold, which perishes even though refined by fire – may result in praise, glory and honour when Jesus Christ in revealed (1 Peter 1:6-7).

Thank you God, for showing us the good, such that we won't dwell on the bad. Thank you for giving us just enough strength for the day. Thank you Jesus...no matter our pain, you have known worse, and you overcame so that we might know life. Thank you God for your promise that no valley is too dark for your light to shine, and no sky too grey for a rainbow.

Thank you, Sue, for encouraging us to write our story, Joshua's story.

Be strong and courageous for I will be with you wherever you go (Joshua 1:9).

Mark and Holly Bowtell

*****

Having read these stories, I'm sure you have been so moved by the courage these dear souls have had, to share with you their most sad and difficult times in their lives. Why did they agree to my request to share them in this book? To make themselves vulnerable and relive the moments as they were brought to the surface again?

So that if we are faced with circumstances that are insurmountable, we too may find a way to press through with God and find the hidden gems in our dark places.

Have you ever been in a dark room and shone a torch onto a diamond ring? All around is dark and as the rays of light hit the diamond, it illuminates its many facets, twinkling and shining its beauty.

So it is with God as we reflect on these poignant heart-moving stories we have just read. That is exactly what He has done for these dear souls. He has turned their darkness by coming into their pain and grief, revealing His treasures that reflect His goodness and love.

Challenge:

Have you the courage to ask the Lord to loosen that deep splinter of immeasurable pain in your heart so He can heal your heart?

Prayer:

Lord Jesus, give me the courage to face whatever I go through in my journey in life to always remember that You are with me every step of the way and will see me through, however bad the pain is. Amen

13
GOD OF THE SPACIOUS PLACES

He brought me out into a spacious place; he rescued me because he delighted in me (Psalm 18 v19 NIV).

When I first read this passage I felt I was in a prison. Life had closed in on me. The rose-tinted glasses that I had worn were well and truly smashed and I was almost crushed. I must admit to thinking at the time, well that's certainly not for me...there's no way out of this. I'd taken on a role as my dad's main carer thinking I had all the grace and patience I could ever need. Wrong!

I had the past experience of caring for a wonderful husband who was terminally ill with cancer. A precious time mingled with the sadness that would eventually take him from my life.

I had a caring heart and a passion to help people, so surely this new role as a full-time carer for my father would be an equally enriching experience.

There were times especially as I started this role that were pleasant and fulfilling. However, what a shock as the rose-tinted glasses fell to the floor in pieces revealing stark reality.

This might all sound somewhat negative and not really what you'd want to hear. But sadly, this sometimes can be the case when we are stressed, tired and irritated. As Christians, we think we should always have a smile on our face, be always coping victoriously. I hate to shatter that image, but it's not always the case.

The reason I'm sharing this is to help maybe *you* who may feel a failure, that your pristine plans aren't going exactly as you thought. And that pit-sinking feeling envelopes you, bringing the reality that you are in this over your head and there's no way out.

As I looked at the passage at the beginning of the chapter, I must admit my first thought was...oh yes, an escape plan. The word 'rescue' jumped out at me. I imagined a seven-foot angel coming down from Heaven and whisking me to a dream destination (I was hoping the Caribbean) far, far away from the prison I sometimes felt encased in.

I allowed my mind to conjure up wide open spaces without invisible bars encasing me. I breathed in this imaginary vision that my mind had set before me. The reality soon hit me. There was no escape. I was in this to the end.

Yet this passage was clear. He would rescue me, to take me into a spacious place, because He delighted in me. I thought I'm sure He cannot possibly delight in me. I felt a failure in this task He had given me. Yet this was what the passage said; the passage I felt drawn to had resonated deep within my being.

God delighted in me. How could a holy God delight in me when I felt such a failure? How many of us underestimate the effects that lack of sleep, being on call 24 hours a day and for many of us carers, not being appreciated. It can have the most detrimental effect on us. It doesn't happen overnight. We are worn down over a period of time, subtly, like a piece of wood whittled continually.

How many times I wished I was a robot, void of feeling and as long as I was fully charged could perform all the tasks asked of me. Yet, God said in His Word, He delighted in me. He saw my human frailty and understood my every feeling and still loved me, warts and all. It blew my mind! I was so important to Him that He would rest His eyes on His weary daughter and rescue me.

I knew there was no earthly way I could be whisked away by a knight in shining armour because I had committed myself to being my father's full-time carer and wanted to do the very best I could.

So how could God rescue me? As I meditated on this scripture, I began to see the escape plan unfold. My circumstances remained the same, but what I noticed was that my heart began to change in the middle of them. Instead of the crushing, claustrophobic feeling I had experienced, He began to bring a peace into the core of my heart.

The cage that I felt had made me a captive began to be dismantled, bar by bar, enabling me to almost physically breathe more deeply and more freely without restrictions. Yet nothing had changed on the outside. But God had rescued me from the inside. Here was now my spacious place. I could function, love and serve in the place He had chosen for me to do His will.

This scripture kept me buoyant over the following weeks and months. I can't say that every day it was easy, because it wasn't. However, I knew the reality that God would rescue me if it got too much for me, because He delighted in me and He did right up to the end of my father's life.

What a wonderful, awesome promise He has given us in His Word. The good news is that there are so many of these good nuggets tucked into His Word waiting for us to discover and experience the treasure they bring.

Challenge:

Do you feel a captive with no means of escape? Take heart, my friend. God looks down at you and says, 'I understand...I will rescue you and bring you into a spacious place...because I delight in you.' Are you ready to embrace this promise He has for you?

Prayer:

Lord Jesus, I need you to come and break down the prison walls that encompass me. They threaten to suffocate me. I give you permission to come into my heart afresh and do a new work within me that I might know the reality of living in freedom, Your spacious place. Let me shine even here for You, Lord Jesus. Amen.

14
GOD OF ETERNITY

I've been writing this book during the pandemic of Covid-19. Following Covid vaccine availability, lockdowns and social distancing, we have seen fewer people dying and as I speak the variant is less toxic as we approach Spring 2022.

I'm still personally shopping on line, and being very careful. My main link with people has been video chats, Zoom meetings, and phone and garden visits. I look out onto a garden that is producing new life in preparation for the promise of Spring which brings light to a darkened world.

Many of us have had time during this enforced life-changing period to ponder over our lives, our uncertain futures, and reflect over what's important, really important in this materialistic world we live in.

As I shared in my first book, my volunteer work with the chaplaincy is a passion deep within my heart. I miss the work tremendously and feel deprived by Covid-19 restrictions by not being there. However, amongst many home activities I have had the opportunity to use my time to look deeply into my passion of being with the sick and the dying.

As a Christian, I believe God's Word that says He heals. Also that this didn't end in the time of the apostles. Some years ago I myself experienced healing from an overactive thyroid gland that gave me lots of discomfort. This meant that the planned operation no longer needed to take place.

I also know what it is to lose loved ones who have had many prayers of healing offered for them, but they died. Does that mean that God didn't hear our prayers for them? No. He had a bigger, eternal plan for their lives. He took those who believed in Him to Himself and made them whole for ever.

I believe the subject of healing is one of the big mysteries that we have to wait for until Heaven to be fully revealed to us. I've taken time over these past months to understand the changes in attitudes to dying that, even in the 75 years that I've been on this Earth, have changed dramatically.

I was brought up in a modern post-war environment, blessed with adequate housing that accommodated our nuclear family. Grandparents lived separately in their own homes. My mother came from Yorkshire and married a Welsh man. Our maternal grandparents lived in Yorkshire, so we were brought up with only seeing them once or twice a year.

My paternal grandparents lived only a short car ride away, so we visited them regularly. They had the advantage of having a single live-in daughter. She cared for their every need and was able to nurse them at home when they were ill. When they grew old she was able to care for them, allowing them to die in the safety and comfort of their own home because of the sacrificial care by their daughter and the community healthcare workers surrounding them.

As chaplaincy volunteers at Tŷ Olwen, our local hospice, we see patients coming in for system and pain control to get on top of the symptoms that their terminal cancer has placed them with. Sometimes changes have to take place. Perhaps up until then they were capable of seeing to their own hygiene. Mobility might have changed and the trip to the upstairs bathroom and their bedroom is no longer be possible.

The family can no longer avoid the inevitable. A rethink is necessary. This can be a big and painful adjustment as their privacy now has to be invaded. Carers may be needed to provide necessary help each day.

Their well-maintained homes suddenly have to be shuffled around to accommodate the needs of their loved one. No one is really prepared for the invasion that is necessary to take place. But as furniture is dismantled and resited, life begins its new normal, readjustments begin, and love and care warm the heart of patients as they see how important they are. Coming to terms with all these changes takes time, but the benefits of all the effort makes it all worthwhile.

We know that nursing a loved one at home cannot always be possible for many reasons. My mum died in Tŷ Olwen hospice. As a family we had the privilege to care for her in her own home right up to just two weeks before she died.

Although we knew she was terminally ill, we had no idea when she went into the hospice for respite, while my father recovered from an operation, that she would be taken from us within two weeks. Yet we knew that she was in the right place. Her needs had greatly increased and the 24-hour wonderful care she received at the hospice gave her dignity to the end.

When you live alone and can no longer manage, sometimes it means that residential or nursing home care may be necessary. This is not an easy decision, but with the help of community healthcare workers and family, suitable accommodation can be found.

As a carer for my father for many years, I find it strange as the years have rolled on that these may be changes I have to face for myself. As I enter my 75th year and still feel twenty-one in my mind, it's hard to align the two. Yet my body knows it has need for regular MOTs. Creaking, aching joints show signs of wear and tear.

Whether I like it or not, it's inevitable in the ageing process. It's a reality check. I need to face the fact that I may become the person to be cared for and not the role that I have taken for many years – as the carer.

So how do we approach eternity? Many times I have heard it said that it's not the dying people are frightened of, but the process. Nobody embraces these thoughts. Yet we know that if we follow Jesus, He has promised to be with us every step of the way.

The exciting thing is that until our very last breath we are used as His precious instruments to all He sends in our paths. For those of us who have reached or have even passed retirement age, we are not on the scrap heap – far from it.

If we were always activity-driven people, then it can come as quite a shock to us that what was once so easy to manoeuvre, now becomes a real task. The adjustment stage is very necessary to be able to adapt and maybe refocus onto a different way to achieve. We may also have to come to terms with the need to re-evaluate our ministries He has given us over the years.

We have a choice. In the period of adjustment to these changes, we can fight them or make a conscious decision to embrace them. Again I quote the writer Amy Carmichael back in the 1850s, 'In acceptance lieth peace.' It's not passive but active and even a healthy outlook.

In my first book I spoke about my dear friend Babs. Her life over the past few years has been dogged by ever-increasing sickness. After years of hospital admissions for many operations and life-threatening sepsis, she plods on.

Her mobility now is limited. To be able to eat she now has to have her food mashed or blended. She spends most of the night in her chair as that's the only place she can get comfort with her painful joints. Her sleep is punctuated by hours of wakefulness. She has lost her independence and is totally reliant on a wonderfully caring husband.

Has she given up on God? Never. There have been times when it's been dark and lonely but she's held on. Despite her body being less able to function, she has pressed on knowing that God has promised never to leave her or forsake her. What an example to us. I'm sure there have been times when she felt useless and impotent. Gone are the days of doing for others with her many acts of kindness.

Yet her position is probably more effective than ever before. She listens to those who pour out their hearts to her and takes them to the Lord in prayer – surely the most beautiful of all our service to Him.

Challenge:

Are there things in my life that I cannot change yet I fight against them causing me to be weary, frustrated and downcast. Have I the courage to really let them go to the Lord and begin to find that peace that comes from acceptance?

Prayer:

The Serenity Prayer:
God grant me the serenity to accept the things I cannot change,
the courage to change the things I can,
and the wisdom to know the difference.
Dr Reinhold Niebuhr (1892–1971)

15

GOD IN THE EARTHQUAKE

Have you ever lived through an earthquake? You may be surprised to hear this if you live in Swansea.

The headlines of a newspaper on 27th June, 1906, stated, 'An earthquake…great seismic disturbance in South Wales…Swansea thrown into panic this morning…Confusion in the schools…Terror in the homes… Buildings tremble and crack…Magnitude 5.2.' It was the most damaging earthquake to hit Britain during the twentieth century.

As I Googled (good old Google) to learn more about earthquakes in Wales, I was very surprised to know how frequent they were. But generally they are so small that they are hardly felt by us and don't usually affect our lives.

But what about the 'earthquakes' that happen in our own lives? An earthquake in our circumstances that happens in our lives can change in the twinkling of an eye. I think back in my life, and without being a drama queen there have been some real earthquakes that have taken the ground from underneath me.

The first must have been when my dreams of becoming a nurse were shattered as my adolescent frame couldn't stand the pressure and I had a nervous breakdown. This was so unexpected and completely out of my control.

The second was when my first pregnancy was threatened for many months, the birth was traumatic, and a time of devastation as the idyllic picture of a joyous dream coming true was robbed by severe post-natal depression.

The third must have been facing the reality of a marriage that wasn't working with the events that brought it to such an abrupt ending.

Other earthquakes in my life have been facing the trauma of loved ones losing their battles with cancer and other diseases. You might say, 'But this is life,' and you are right. Nevertheless, they are indeed earthquakes in our lives.

We know from the pictures of earthquakes we see in the media that our first sight is of the devastation – homes completely wrecked, rubble, smoke and dust clouds, survivors desperately searching for loved ones. Rescuers arriving to salvage anything or anyone who has not been destroyed. Straining to hear sounds of life from under the rubble.

So many emotions rising to the surface – shock, disbelief, numbness, confusion, anger and hopelessness, to name but a few that dominate each breath that is taken.

I can so identify with these feelings in my own personal earthquakes. So many emotions to process, and like grief they come in no particular order. I had no control or say as my brain brought forth each emotion from within.

Although I must say I think shock must be the first emotion that causes disbelief and numbness. Perhaps we are wired this way in order that we won't explode with the pain of it all.

The scene changes as hours move on…there's a strange, eerie quietness as the dust clouds settle, the debris more visible with the last chance of salvaging anything from what was. The reality of the devastation and life change that this event has caused begins to sink in. Rescuers arrive with compassion and love, willing to help in whatever way they can.

So it is with our own personal earthquake. We reel from the shock and disbelief. We gather ourselves together from the heap that we were reduced to and begin, very slowly, to put one step in front of another as we gingerly place our feet on what we hope is more solid ground. May we have earthly angels sent to us to journey with us and help us pick up the pieces. Slowly, very slowly we begin to rebuild; healing cannot be rushed – it takes precious time requiring so much energy and often redirection in our lives.

The same happens with the earthquakes on our planet. The ground has first to settle, then completely cleared of the debris. It has to be made safe again. Planning and rebuilding can begin too. It is rarely ever exactly the same. Structurally they have extra strength. Sometimes the area is changed forever and becomes a place of memorial and reminders. It becomes tranquil with nature and creation allowed to bloom and flourish as a reminder of fresh hope... beauty from the ashes.

One thing is for sure – we are never the same. As we heal we have the opportunity to build in new strengths which enable us to begin to have courage to move forward. This may mean a new direction, making changes that give us new calibre that comes forth.

In all this we must never underestimate God's power in us, from the beginning of the devastation that the earthquake has brought us to the healing power by His Holy Spirit to become restored. It is a process. Time is necessary for full healing to take place. Our scars may always be visible, but in time they stop causing us pain. We can use them to remember how God brought us through what was one of the most painful times in our lives to a place of victory.

Never underestimate His love for us. We may not feel it at the time of the terrible darkness earthquakes cause in our lives, but be reassured, the darkness will diminish. Light will break through and hope will be the incentive to carry on.

Grace and peace to you from God our Father and the Lord Jesus Christ...who comforts us in all our troubles, so that we can comfort those in any trouble with the comfort we ourselves have received from God (2 Corinthians 1 v2-4).

Challenge:

Can you trust God with the earthquakes that you've hidden deep within your heart and bring them into His light for His healing touch?

Prayer:

Lord God, I choose to trust You with my devastating earthquakes that have shaped my life and often distorted it. Please place Your healing hand upon them and set me free so that my ashes may be turned into Your beauty so I may give You all the glory. Amen.

16
GOD IN CREATIVITY

What could be more spectacular than the season of Spring to write on creativity.

As the Spring of 2021 began to burst forth with colour and light following the greyness of the winter and Covid restrictions throughout the world, it felt like hope had at last dawned upon us.

Probably most of us embraced this season as never before. Restrictions had affected all of us. Some of us felt deprived after nearly a year of trying to live in the 'new normal' social distancing and staying at home during the lockdown times.

Online shopping for most of our goods, giving everything that came through our doors a wipe over with an anti-bacterial tissue. Not being able to visit families, travel on holiday and at times not being allowed to even share company in one's own garden with a friend. A bleak, dark, isolating time for so many.

So Spring is being a real gift to us. The courageous snowdrops lifting their heads through frost and snowflakes. The daffodils waving their bright yellow trumpets in the cool winds, the crocuses and primroses adding to the master beauty of this season of splendour.

I don't know if you're anything like me, but I still marvel at creation. God, the Creator, sharing with us humans His creation. Take the butterfly. To gaze at the open wings of a butterfly getting its nourishment on a leaf in a garden. The incredible symmetrical and intricate detail on its wings. God wasn't satisfied by making just one type He designed approximately eighteen thousand species. Can you imagine eighteen thousand species!

But isn't that just like God. His giving to us is without measure. This is just a glimpse of what is to come for our eternity in Heaven. I hope there are butterflies there.

What about our creativity? If you were anything like me when I was asked in school to create something, I felt I was expected to be a master artist, which I certainly was not. So I never thought I was a creative being. I was hopeless at music and could only play a recorder, very much out of tune.

I've since learnt from that thought of many years ago what it means to make something new and somehow valuable, and it broadened my understanding.

I knew I didn't have a flair with drawing; my proportions were never right, and to be honest it didn't bring me pleasure. I knew that certainly wasn't a gifting for me.

My love for beautiful scenes, sunrises and sunsets, His beautiful nature, especially flowers, led me to begin to enjoy basic photography. I found as I captured that moment that I was able to preserve it in a photograph.

As time moved on, we entered the digital era when we could simply snap away in amateur mode and simply delete any shots that weren't worth keeping. It was easy then to store them on a device and share them with a friend without the process of having to have them developed.

Do you remember the time when you excitedly ran into the shop to collect the printed type only to find you'd taken a whole reel of film without removing the lens cap, or that finger had got in the way, or light had got into the camera and ruined the whole reel? I wonder if in generations to come photo albums will come back into fashion? Time will tell.

I remember when cross stitching became the craze. I really got into this. I made cards, pictures and little items to give as gifts. I felt pleased that I could create something special from embroidery threads and the cross stitch fabric and patterns.

Some years later a lovely Godly lady from Singapore had prayed over me and she felt that was going to give me a gift of creativity. At the time it was quite difficult for me as I was a full-time carer with little spare time. Nevertheless she persisted in praying and repeated many times to me that God was going to give me this gift of creativity bigger than I could ever imagine. To be honest I wanted to laugh as it seemed absurd. But God's timing isn't ours. Years later this has happened in most wonderful and joyful ways.

He led and provided me to renovate the home I now live in so I could provide a short-term rest for weary ladies. After some years and circumstances, the vision changed shape and I was able to provide day care for weary ladies. At the start we had a craft afternoon which was such fun as we learnt to be creative with one another.

I remember my dear friend and artist Dawn Fisher encouraging us saying not to compare our work with one another's; enjoy what you're doing and then it's always successful. So true. This gives new confidence to press on to explore and develop often dormant gifts.

All this built in me confidence to trust God and enjoy creating little gifts with fabrics and my sewing machine. This book will have benefited from some items that I have sold to help with the funding.

Why am I labouring this point? The very reason is I want you to look at your creativity that might not have been tapped into. Do you feel you don't have this gift? That God dished it out and there wasn't any left for you? Not true! Everyone of us has the potential to exercise this gift if we are just willing to have a go.

When I first opened as a respite, I incorporated into the activities I could provide each day an art and craft time. There would be opportunities to try new things card making, mosaic, sketching, watercolour or acrylic painting, pebble painting, to name but a few. Never underestimate the therapeutic value of such activities.

When a person has a heavy heart and a counselling situation might scare them, how much easier it is for some as they sit together creating something with their hands, knowing they are being heard and listened to in a safe place, which is both cathartic and healing.

As we seek to encourage those around us, we can help to develop the gift of creativity in their lives. Art and craft therapy has the potential to lower stress levels. Engaging with the task in hand releases the heavy heart for at least that period of time. The sense of achievement has such an effect on us. It has the potential to lift us from the gloom, taps us on the back and brings a lightness to our hearts.

As I think back to the different ladies who have come through the doors of Shalom4 sometimes with heavy, breaking hearts, I have seen God do the most amazing things as they see the art and craft table set before them to pick something they would enjoy having a go at.

It's as if they walk away from their heavy hearts and enter into the joy-task set before them, like a child delighting in the prospects of creating something potentially beautiful. I notice the worry lines in their faces disappear, the smile on their lips begin to break through and a delight as they see what they themselves have created. Isn't that just so wonderful!

It's like God gets them to focus on something that brings them joy while He pours His healing balm upon their broken hearts. Just wonderful.

For me, as they leave after just a few days of respite and TLC, it was always so very rewarding and faith-building to see the beginning of a future and hope once again in their lives.

To close this chapter may I add this. You have read 'Judith's story' in a previous chapter. She has been given a word that God wants her to continue with the gift He has given her in her creativity. We marvel at her now up-and-running studio as she becomes a business, prepared to serve the Lord in her creativity and using the profits to help the work of eating disorders.

Maybe it's time for you to start something new. Dust off the pallet and paints that are tucked in the back of a cupboard waiting for an opportunity to be used again. Or maybe your sewing machine is ready and waiting for you. Or catching creation in nature by taking pictures of Spring blooms, ocean scenes and the beauty captured by a camera?

Challenge:

Are you ready to embark on a new way of creativity in your life? Have you long desired creative interests that you've never had time for? Maybe this is the time to begin for yourself or for others who God brings alongside you on this journey.

Prayer:

Lord Jesus, thank You for Your gift of creativity. Help me to develop what You have given me for me to glorify You and help others to find their creative gifting. Amen.

17

GOD OF GRACE

As I sat pondering the possible contents of this chapter. A big ball of wool on my lap that had become unruly and as if having a mind of its own had become a tangled mess! I looked down upon it and wondered about spending the next hour carefully untangling it with sheer determination that it was not getting the better of me. When I thought I had beaten it, this rebellious ball of wool split apart and became almost as bad as it was when I started. I decided to stick with it and complete the task in hand to tame it.

What's this got to do with grace you may ask? As I occupied my hands with the tedious yet compelling task of untangling the wool, my mind was free to meditate on the start of this chapter headed 'grace'.

As my fingers weaved in and out of the tangled mess and a new ball of wool began to form, I thought of our lives in the hands of our Heavenly Father. He comes to us. So often our lives are like this tangled mess that lay in my hands.

But let's first talk about what grace is…

Grace is undeserved favour, God's mercy towards mankind. It is not a created substance of any kind; it is an attribute of God that is most manifest in the salvation of sinners. An attribute of God, the very nature of God. He longs to bestow His grace upon every created being. We cannot physically see it, feel it even, yet it has a profound life-changing effect on our lives into eternity.

Grace and mercy are intertwined together, for they are ongoing in our lives after receiving the grace of God in His redeeming love at the forgiveness of our sins. We humans are slow to learn and very often slip back into our carnal ways, needing God's grace and mercy to restore us once again. To receive His grace is the most amazing, profound gift we can ever receive while we are living on this planet. We can have the most desired material things showered upon us, but they fall short of the pure beauty of God's grace.

I recently read this question about grace: is it fair? I reflected on this – grace being unfair. How could this possibly be? It dawned on me how from our perspective grace could be unfair. We are ready to receive the gift and epiphany moment of receiving this precious gift, but when it comes to 'giving grace', that can be a different story.

What happens when we are confronted to give grace and mercy and even forgiveness to an abusive partner, a bullying boss, unkind family or friends, to name a few? We are quick to make a case in the defence that this isn't something that grace and mercy can do. But as lovely as grace and mercy are life-changing to us, we need to extend it to others. This isn't easy.

When our hearts have been broken, flashed-back memories invade our emotions causing pain and keep us limping around inside. If God is healing us from past hurts and pains, we are often challenged with extending grace and mercy, even when we protest that they don't deserve it!

We cannot help but go back to when we were saturated with God's love and kindness in the form of His mercy and grace. Did we deserve to be forgiven and loved? Yet He still poured out His love and grace upon us. So we must too.

You may say, 'But how can I do this; those who hurt me are no longer living,' or 'I couldn't go to them even though I want to forgive them.' The good news is the willingness to let God, through His grace, forgive them. This is a process, and at this stage it's words. You may find lots of hidden, painful memories begin to surface. God does that when He's bringing out your pains and suffering in order to bring lasting healing.

This is about His love for you. It's about your freedom. I have always found this practical way helps to take this forward. Write the person a letter. I say here that this will probably not ever get sent. Set time aside to be able to reflect. You might have been journalling your thoughts as God has been bringing things to the surface. Write this letter from your pain, from your heart, say it as it is, and when you have finished, offer it to God. Ask for His grace and mercy to cover it. In a safe place set it alight and know that God has seen every word you have written and has taken it to heal your heart and bring you new freedom.

There have been times in my life when in my mind dropped the scripture, *My grace is sufficient for you* (2 Corinthians 12v9 NIV). I must confess on one occasion curled up in the corner of a room in a fetal position ranting at God saying, 'Oh no it's not!' At that very moment I could not see past the circumstances and the desperate hopelessness I was feeling. I forgot that I was just seeing the situation at that very second, not how He was going to work it through. The verse continues, '…for my power is made perfect in weakness.' How often we can forget to add this second part and see it in context. I most certainly was weak.

Within hours He had taken the situation and turned it around. I remember even being able to laugh that very same evening as I saw His grace come in and change me. He simply asks us to trust Him. He will give us no more than we can take. That's grace, His grace.

There have been thousands of words written about grace, far better than I ever could. I hope I've caught the essence of grace for you as you read this chapter.

Challenge:

Thank God for outpouring His grace and mercy upon you. Is the Lord showing you that there are some parts of your heart that need a grace touch from Him? Can you trust Him to listen to your heart and your pain in order to heal you?

Prayer:

God of grace and mercy, I give you permission to search my heart for anything that has been hidden that I need to be set free from by the power of Your love, grace and mercy. Help me to let go and let You pour Your healing balm over all my pain of the past hurts and set me free. In Jesus' Name, Amen.

18

GOD OF THE HEDGEHOGS

I make no excuses for writing this very short chapter probably the shortest you've ever read. So here goes.

Hedgehogs. What can they possibly have to do with butterflies? They may be cute to look at and preservation of this species is admirable, but they certainly aren't a cuddly pet. Their spines can pierce human skin, causing infections and some nasty diseases. They even eat butterflies! What if you long to be a beautiful, graceful butterfly, but see yourself as a spine-filled hedgehog prickly, brown and unattractive? I've got great news for you; God loves hedgehogs as much as butterflies!

I was reflecting on some words a friend said of how she felt like a hedgehog. She so often would find herself going into a defence mode when in a challenging situation, aware that she often felt irritated and out of place. She would long to retreat in time before the spines would emerge to protect herself, often causing a sense of failure or guilt. Yet deep in her heart she longed to be that beautiful, colourful butterfly. Does that mean there's no hope for her? Certainly not.

Is this you? If it is, the wonderful news is that God has His hands open wide for you. No need to project those spines any more. He longs to heal hearts from past pains. To transform you as you trust in Him. This may sound very simplistic. It's not a quick fix, I know, but our loving and gracious God longs to heal us, to set us free, to be whole as He intended. You too can have beautiful butterfly wings that are vibrant with an array of unimaginable colours; to fly in a freedom you've never experienced.

Docs that mean we'll never feel like a hedgehog again? I wish I could say yes, but the truth is that we're human and can slip back if we rely on our own strength and ways. We need to rely on the Holy Spirit daily to give us a fresh filling so that we grow more like Jesus day by day.

Challenge:
Are we willing to let God carefully pick us up, prickles and all, and begin the work of changing us to be more like Jesus?

Prayer:
Holy Spirit, fall afresh on me. I give You permission to take the hedgehog me, take away all that's made me prickle, and change me into a beautiful butterfly so that I may shine in glorious colour for You, giving You all the Glory. Amen.

19
GOD OF OUR MEMORIES

I smugly began to relax as I emailed the first draft of this book, *Butterfly Wings*, to my proofreader. I knew from my last book that it would be like a game of squash, back and forth, as we corrected, edited, and aligned in readiness for its publication. But nevertheless I had that contentment that the first hurdle of a book with framework was now under my belt.

In a random, jovial dialogue with my church house group we call 'Circles', I realised that I had to add this chapter. After all, the very conception of this sequel book was the sense that I had that the Lord wanted me to write by drawing from my memories.

In Psalm 139, David writes that we are fearfully and wonderfully made. I did some research on which part of the brain our memories are stored. It seems that explicit memories are stored in the hippocampus, neocortex and the amygdala. How amazing is our God to make us so intricate.

Forgive me if I've already shared some of the following in *This is My Story, This is My Song.*

Each one of us has memories. Some of us, for various reasons, may have difficulty recalling certain things. One reason could be because of trauma in our lives, and our mind has blocked out painful memories. Some are bittersweet.

I remember when as a teenager my faithful cat Timmy, my lovely furry companion I'd grown up with, died of what must have been old age. It was the first time I'd encountered losing someone. I can still remember the grief of parting with him. It has been etched in my memory.

I vividly recall the devastation when my first marriage fell apart and I was temporarily homeless. My family was split up. My home, lovingly put together and cherished for so many years, was no more. An earthquake had happened. My security had been blown into oblivion.

I entered a new world that included places I'd never been before. A scary world...the DHSS system, as I now needed benefits. On a list for emergency housing. A world that was so alien to me. To gather just a few personal possessions stacked in a carport and start again. To face divorce and all its effects on the family. To marry again and find happiness that was only to last for twelve years when cancer took him away from me. To lose both my grandmothers, one to cancer; then my mum and sister lost their battle with cancer.

That's a bit of a list of losses isn't it…but where was God in all this? Sad, hard memories, but that wasn't the end of them. God was in the centre of every one.

He brought the Cheedy family alongside me in those dark days of my marriage breakup. They walked the journey with me, every step of the way. I was emergency housed within the month and through the generosity of family and friends I was lacking nothing. Everything was provided for me to make a home.

As these memories flood back in my mind they don't hurt and sting as they did back then because God was with me in those times. He provided for me in the most incredible ways as I journeyed on through the twists and turns of life as a single parent. Bittersweet, filled with His loving kindness. And because of that, my memory is healed.

The way God brought my second husband, Ron, into my life. What a shock for me. I certainly had no intentions of getting married again. But God had other ideas!

In the most amazing series of events, He orchestrated our meeting and led us very quickly through a pathway that brought us into marriage. I was loved and cherished for twelve years by this dear man. Strange as it may seem, it was as if I knew that I wasn't to have him in my life for decades.

He became ill very early on in our marriage which eventually led to his cancer journey that finally took him from me. He loved Jesus and I knew He was in Heaven rejoicing with His Saviour, and free from pain and sorrow. We both knew God walked closely with us through every second of our twelve years together. My memories are always there and I can recall the happy and sad times we experienced together, and they are mingled with the joy that we were never alone. We walked with God through it all.

My Welsh grandmother had become a Christian in the Welsh Revival of 1904. When she was coming to the end of her life during my first marriage, there was an incident that was very significant to me at the time.

I was struggling with faith issues. I'd always believed in God but knew there was something always missing. It was a period of eleven months of what I can clearly describe as 'God instances' in my life; they were far above any coincidences.

My grandmother, I called Nanna, was very ill and nearing the end of her life. She was at home and lovingly looked after by her daughter Betty. At the time my aunt and mum had fallen out and were estranged. This bothered me immensely.

As I travelled to visit my Nanna, who lived a few miles away, my mode of transport in those days was a Moped. Halfway through my journey I heard a voice that was so clear in my mind saying to tell my aunt to read out the Lord's Prayer! Nothing like this had ever happened to me before.

I felt without a doubt that this was God speaking. When I arrived I told my aunt what had happened. We sat down and she spoke out the words of the Lord's Prayer. When we got to the bit that says, 'forgive those who trespass against us', she broke down and asked forgiveness from God and chose to forgive my mum.

Within twenty-four hours my Nanna passed away peacefully. I knew that despite her not knowing the feud that was going on between sisters-in-law, she'd hung on until there was reconciliation. Her death was a healing death. A memory for me is that God's love and faithfulness never ends, as my new awesome journey began knowing Jesus as my personal Saviour.

I have had the privilege that God unlocked the many painful memories in His time and when He knew I was ready. We know that we cannot take away what has happened to us. However, with God it is possible to have those memories put safely in His hands and have them bathed and soothed to a place where they can no longer hold us prisoner of the hurts they caused us.

Many years ago a lovely young lady stayed with me and I knew she had many traumatic memories that were so painful locked inside her that kept her a prisoner. She was totally unaware of the devastating abuse that had taken place. When the time was right, God led her to a book called *Silent Scream*. As she read it, God opened her heart and mind to what had taken place, and in the safety of His Love and healing hands, He ministered to her and set her free from the past for ever.

Just the other evening as I recalled some sad memories, I found them taken to a place of joy   the time I was homeless to the time of holidaying in the Caribbean.

You see, we have a God of the impossible! As we trust Him with every aspect of our lives, our journeys are daily enriched by His love, grace and mercy.

From our times of desolation to the times of great joy, it's only God who can do that for us, ministering His grace into our conscious and subconscious memories and lifting us from the cage that has imprisoned us to a place where we can fly like a beautiful butterfly.

Challenge:

Is this the very time that God is calling you to His side

for the healing of your memories that have imprisoned you? Are you ready to forgive those who have imprinted lasting sad memories in your life?

Prayer:

Lord Jesus, I know You are a safe place and I am ready to bring my unhealed memories before You. I give you permission to take my heart, take my memories and heal them, Lord. Let me fly like that beautiful butterfly in all its beautiful splendour. Amen

20

BUTTERFLY WINGS – READY TO FLY

So, dear reader, congratulations that you haven't put the book down yet! My prayer for you is that through the words on each page, God has been giving your wings fresh colour. He may have brightened up the colour that had gone dusty and grey. He may have even changed a dull and dark colour into something new and vibrant.

Whatever He has done, I pray that He has brought you to a new place.

Indulge me for a moment. Shut your eyes…and in your mind's eye see yourself as a butterfly, held gently on an open hand of your Creator. Feel His gentle stroke as He bathes and cleans all that has made your wings colourless. See Him reach for His pallet and carefully mix unique and beautiful colours especially created just for you.

With each brushstroke of exquisite colours, watch Him mirror the identical markings on the other wing, every line and shape created and perfected just for you. He stands back and admires His handiwork. He delights in what He sees.

He extends His hand and the butterfly edges to the end of His fingers and opens its wings to display such splendour of magnificent colour, and with full confidence soars in the air with boldness and beauty.

And that's what He wants to do for you! He is healing you to fly and soar again: in fact to take you to heights you've not yet discovered. Don't miss this opportunity. Trust Him, fly and soar as never before!

Isaiah 40:31 NIV

But those who hope in the Lord will renew their strength. They will soar on wings like eagles; they will run and not grow weary, they will walk and not be faint.

####

If you enjoyed this book, please leave a review on Amazon. You may like to read the first book:

Sue Williams has written this book in response to a word God clearly gave her: ***Tell of what I have done for you***. The scripture He gave her was from Psalm 9: *I'm thanking you God from a full heart. I'm writing the book of your wonders. I'm whistling, laughing and jumping for joy. I'm singing your song, High God.* (The Message)

May you be encouraged and even challenged to launch out into the deep, abandoning your comfort zone, setting your sails to new horizons as you embrace the love and provision of Jesus in a way you never thought possible. I promise you that if you do, you will never be the same…

This is My Story, This is My Song - reviewed in the United Kingdom on 23rd November 2020.

This is a beautiful account of the joys and trials of an ordinary life, lived for a higher purpose. Sue's story demonstrates the immeasurably positive impact on others, of a life lived in simple obedience to God. Sue's experience of following Jesus in a context of much suffering and loss is authentic, powerful and overwhelmingly inspirational. Sue speaks with such passion and energy, a gently challenging but genuinely motivational read. Thank you, Sue, for being faithful to God's call on your life, and for sharing yourself so generously with others, in reality, and within the pages of this book. It's been a joy. I eagerly await the sequel!

Jan M.

Printed in Great Britain
by Amazon